REDEMPTION HISTOR

For the arguments behind my comments in this volume, in addition to the relevant articles and video clips, see my:

Assurance in the New Covenant.

Baptist Sacramentalism: A Warning to Baptists.

Battle For The Church 1517-1644.

Believers under the Law of Christ.

Christ is All: No Sanctification by the Law.

Conversion Ruined: The New Perspective and the Conversion of Sinners.

Fivefold Sanctification.

Four 'Antinomians' Tried and Vindicated: Tobias Crisp, William Dell, John Eaton and John Saltmarsh.

Infant Baptism Tested.

Positional Sanctification: Two Consequences.

Romans 11: A Suggested Exegesis.

Sanctification in Galatians.

The Hinge in Romans 1 – 8: A critique of N.T.Wright's view of Baptism and Conversion.

The Essential Sabbath.

The Priesthood of All Believers: Slogan or Substance?

Introduction

In March 2016, I was privileged to be the speaker at the Grace Bible Church Spring Conference, Olive Branch, Mississippi, where I addressed the subject of 'Redemption History Through Covenants'. It occurred to me at the time that my four sessions might be turned into a short book on what I, as a new-covenant theologian,[1] see as the biblical view of the history of redemption through covenants, a book which might introduce this very important topic to some who have not considered it. A little later, I was further moved in this direction by my good friend, Paul A.Kaiser, who wrote to me suggesting that one of the recorded addresses he had heard would make a suitable publication. Even before that, the very warm reception I received at Olive Branch encouraged me much at the time, and I hope that those who heard the original addresses may find this volume a happy reminder of that occasion.[2] More, I hope it will prove useful in the spread of the truth of the gospel. For, make no mistake, that is what we are talking about.

Let me say at once, however, that there are bigger, fuller, more detailed works on covenant history than what you have here. I was trying to get a quart into a pint pot at the conference, and although, in publishing the material for a wider audience, I could have expanded those four addresses into a much larger volume, I decided to limit my publication in the hope that it might, by reason of its smallness, prove more

---

[1] Although I am what is known as a new-covenant theologian, this, in a sense, is unfortunate. I do not wish to be labelled. But labels are here to stay and are fixed to us whether we like it or not. In any case, as I will explain, every believer is a new-covenant theologian – or ought to be!

[2] For those who would like to hear or see the addresses at the Olive Branch Conference, they are available as audios and videos under the following internet links: http://www.gracemessenger.com/sermons/by-serries.html?tag=Redemptive+History+Through+Covenants&key=seri es and on my sermonaudio.com and youtube.com pages.

generally useful to a greater number.[3] At least, that is my prayer in producing and distributing this book.

What are we talking about? What is a covenant?

A covenant is an arrangement by which God deals with men.

And what is redemption?

Redemption speaks of deliverance by purchase; in particular, the sacrifice of Christ to deliver the elect from slavery, the slavery of sin in all its aspects.

Of course, all believers believe in covenants, whether they are dispensationalists, covenant or new-covenant theologians;[4] that is to say, they all use the word 'covenant'. In that sense, therefore, they are all 'covenant theologians', as they should be. After all, the Bible has a great deal to say about both 'covenant' and 'redemption'. And the two are intimately connected. Consequently, all believers must come to terms with the covenant history of redemption. Granted, then, that they all talk about 'covenant', but that, alas, is where unanimity on this subject collapses. The fact is, while all the groups I have mentioned use the word 'covenant', they regard covenant history in very different ways. As a result, redemption history through covenants is yet another bone of contention among believers. This is a serious disagreement. In brief compass in this book I want to set out what I consider to be this history of redemption. I speak for no one else. This is simply how I see things.

But before we go any further, and qualifying what I have just said, let me make this point as clearly as I can: I did not address this conference, nor have I written this book, in order to peddle new-covenant theology. I do not want to be known as a man who tries to sell any system. Rather, my desire and purpose is, as Paul expressed it:

---

[3] I have added a chapter on the Davidic covenant, and some Appendices to amplify certain points.

[4] I am not forgetting progressive dispensationalists or progressive covenantalists. A little more about both of them later.

how can it be anything other than the theology of the new covenant? So then, every believer should be a new-covenant theologian!

Let me now turn to another vital biblical principle of interpretation:

The Old Testament must be interpreted by the New, and not the other way round.

Too many go badly astray at this point. Some treat the Bible as a flat book; the Reformers did, and covenant theologians still do. Some read the New Testament in the light of the Old; that is, they funnel huge tracts of the prophetic writings into the New. Both these approaches are wrong, and wrong scripturally speaking. We should interpret the Old by what we are told in the New. For this, we have Christ's warrant. This is such an important point, let me take a moment or two to explain.

Just before his crucifixion, Christ promised his disciples the gift of the Spirit, speaking first of his work as regards the unbeliever:

> Now I am going to him who sent me... [and] because I have said these things to you, sorrow has filled your heart. Nevertheless, I tell you the truth: it is to your advantage that I go away, for if I do not go away, the Helper will not come to you. But if I go, I will send him to you. And when he comes, he will convict the world concerning sin and righteousness and judgement: concerning sin, because they do not believe in me; concerning righteousness, because I go to the Father, and you will see me no longer; concerning judgement, because the ruler of this world is judged (John 16:5-11).

But the Lord immediately went on to speak of the work of the Spirit with regard to believers:

> I still have many things to say to you, but you cannot bear them now. When the Spirit of truth comes, he will guide you into all the truth, for he will not speak on his own authority, but whatever he hears he will speak, and he will declare to you the things that are to come. He will glorify me, for he will take what is mine and declare it to you. All that the Father has is mine; therefore I said that he will take what is mine and

declare it to you... I have said these things to you in figures of speech. The hour is coming when I will no longer speak to you in figures of speech but will tell you plainly about the Father (John 16:12-15,25).

And he made the same point in his prayer which immediately followed:

I made known to them your name, and I will continue to make it known (John 17:26).

Thus, in short compass, we have a statement of massive import. First, Jesus set his stamp of authority on the apostolic ministry committed to writing, asserting that that ministry would be of 'what is mine', and stating, moreover, that this complete and final revelation would no longer be in shadow and figure but in plain language. Now where would the apostles find 'what is mine'? There would be three aspects to this:

1. The apostles would find 'what is mine' written in the old covenant which they would now be able to understand by the Spirit's enlightenment. Immediately following his resurrection, when speaking with the two disciples on the way to Emmaus, Christ made it clear that he is to be found in the law and the prophets.

2. The apostles would also find 'what is mine' in the things Christ said while he was with them in his earthly ministry.

3. Further, the Spirit would give the apostles 'what is mine' by means of new revelation from Christ after his resurrection.

It is the first aspect which concerns us here. The apostles would find 'what is mine' written in the Old Testament, which they would now be able to read through new-covenant eyes, and thus understand by the Spirit's enlightenment. And herein lies the warrant for saying that we must read the Old Testament (or old covenant) in the light of the New (or new), *and not the other way round*. Above all, we should look for Christ in all the Scriptures, including the Old Testament. As I have noted, Christ immediately confirmed all this when, on the very day of his resurrection, he addressed the two on the road to Emmaus:

God's overall purpose worked out in progressive revelation which has an inbuilt, God-designed discontinuity.

It is in this conviction that I now set out the basic elements of that biblical teaching. And I stress 'basic'. I am setting out a simple outline only – simple but not, I hope, simplistic. I am going to quote Scripture at large and make a few passing comments. For my full arguments upon all the matters I raise, please see my other works.

In order to be as helpful as possible, I will make use of an illustration throughout this work. Imagine the laying of a table for a meal. Picture the tablecloth, the cutlery, the napkins, the glasses and plates. And then there is the menu, illustrated with photographs as well as descriptions of the food to come. And then we have the actual meal itself. This is the illustration I shall be calling on throughout this work.

Scripture shows us that God has revealed and accomplished the redemption of his elect by means of various covenants – different covenants, contrasting covenants, but all progressing according to God's plan, his mind, will, eternal decree, his determined and prophesied purpose. Which is? The culmination and climax of this history of redemption through covenants is to be found in Christ and the new covenant, through which he brings all the elect of all ages in one body to eternal glory.

Finally, to get an overview of what is to come, we can do no better than to read Acts 7. Note how, when Stephen was attacked and tried for the gospel, he started his defence with Abraham:

> Brothers and fathers, hear me. The God of glory appeared to our father Abraham when he was in Mesopotamia, before he lived in Haran, and said to him...

He then moved on to Moses:

> ...who was in the congregation in the wilderness with the angel who spoke to him at Mount Sinai, and with our fathers. He received living oracles to give to [Israel]...

And then David:

...who found favour in the sight of God and asked to find a dwelling place for the God of Jacob. But it was Solomon who built a house for him. Yet the Most High does not dwell in houses made by hands, as the prophet says: 'Heaven is my throne, and the earth is my footstool. What kind of house will you build for me, says the Lord, or what is the place of my rest? Did not my hand make all these things?'

And, as Stephen declared, it all culminated in:

... the coming of the Righteous One [Christ]...

Here it all is: God, in his sovereignty, working out his eternal purpose to save his elect, revealing that redemption by means of covenants in connection with Abraham, Moses, David and then, finally, Christ. In short, Stephen offered his defence in asserting the gospel by preaching the history of redemption revealed through covenants. And this is how we shall now proceed.

him and to him are all things. To him be glory forever. Amen
(Rom. 9:6 – 11:36).

No wonder, then, that the apostle could close his letter to the
Romans with another thunderous declaration of praise:

> Now to him who is able to strengthen you according to my
> gospel and the preaching of Jesus Christ, according to the
> revelation of the mystery[3] that was kept secret for long ages
> but has now been disclosed and through the prophetic writings
> has been made known to all nations, according to the
> command of the eternal God, to bring about the obedience of
> faith – to the only wise God be glory for evermore through
> Jesus Christ! Amen (Rom. 16:25-27).

Opening his letter to the Ephesians, Paul laid down the
foundation for all he intended to say, doing so in the
unchangeable will of God:

> Blessed be the God and Father of our Lord Jesus Christ, who
> has blessed us in Christ with every spiritual blessing in the
> heavenly places, even as he chose us in him *before the
> foundation of the world*, that we should be holy and blameless
> before him. In love he predestined us for adoption as sons
> through Jesus Christ, *according to the purpose of his will*, to
> the praise of his glorious grace, with which he has blessed us
> in the Beloved. In him we have redemption through his blood,
> the forgiveness of our trespasses, according to the riches of his

---

[3] 'Mystery' does not mean 'something mysterious'. Rather, it speaks
of a secret which cannot be grasped or known except by revelation
externally in Scripture *and* inwardly by the Spirit. God did reveal the
mystery in the prophetic writings, but, until the Spirit illuminated the
mind, nobody could understand it. (The same could be said in the
present tense). See Rom. 16:25-27. Witness the number of times
Christ told his disciples of his sufferings and resurrection (Luke
9:22,44-45; 13:33; 18:31-34; 20:9-15; 22:15,22) and yet they failed to
understand it, even after the resurrection (Luke 24:6-7,19-27,
especially verse 25; John 20:9)! The Jews certainly did not understand
the prophets: 'Those who live in Jerusalem and their rulers, because
they did not recognise [Christ] nor understand the utterances of the
prophets, which are read every sabbath, fulfilled them by condemning
him' (Acts 13:27); they 'acted in ignorance' (Acts 3:17). See also
Luke 23:34; John 15:21; 1 Tim. 1:13 with Acts 26:9.

grace, which he lavished upon us, in all wisdom and insight making known to us *the mystery of his will, according to his purpose*, which he set forth in Christ as *a plan for the fullness of time*, to unite all things in him, things in heaven and things on earth. In him we have obtained an inheritance, having been predestined according to the purpose of him who works all things *according to the counsel of his will*, so that we who were the first to hope in Christ might be to the praise of his glory. In him you also, when you heard the word of truth, the gospel of your salvation, and believed in him, were sealed with the promised Holy Spirit, who is the guarantee of our inheritance until we acquire possession of it, to the praise of his glory (Eph. 1:3-14).

Mystery! God's eternal plan! Paul could say of this mystery:

The mystery was made known to me by revelation, as I have written briefly. When you read this, you can perceive my insight into the mystery of Christ, which was not made known to the sons of men in other generations as it has now been revealed to his holy apostles and prophets by the Spirit. This mystery is that the Gentiles are fellow-heirs, members of the same body, and partakers of the promise in Christ Jesus through the gospel. Of this gospel I was made a minister according to the gift of God's grace, which was given me by the working of his power. To me, though I am the very least of all the saints, this grace was given, to preach to the Gentiles the unsearchable riches of Christ, and to bring to light for everyone what is the plan of the mystery hidden for ages in God who created all things, so that through the church the manifold wisdom of God might now be made known to the rulers and authorities in the heavenly places. This was according to the eternal purpose that he has realised in Christ Jesus our Lord (Eph. 3:3-11).[4]

Thus, as every believer can triumphantly exclaim:

God... saved us and called us to a holy calling, not because of our works but because of his own purpose and grace, which he gave us in Christ Jesus before the ages began, and which now has been manifested through the appearing of our Saviour

---

[4] See also Col. 1:27.

promises included physical blessings in the land he had already appointed for possession by the children of Israel after their deliverance from Egypt.

But... was that all? Indeed, was that the great underlying purpose of this covenant with Abraham? Far from it. As always, the New Testament must interpret the Old – not the other way round. And the New Testament makes it plain that the Abrahamic covenant had far more within it than land for the nation of Israel, the possession of which depended on physical descent being ratified by the rite of circumcision. But long before we get to the New Testament, very soon after the original promise, God was telling Abraham that there would be a clear distinction, even within his physical line of descent:

> Abraham said to God: 'Oh that Ishmael might live before you!' God said: 'No, but Sarah your wife shall bear you a son, and you shall call his name Isaac. I will establish my covenant with him as an everlasting covenant for his offspring after him. As for Ishmael, I have heard you; behold, I have blessed him and will make him fruitful and multiply him greatly. He shall father twelve princes, and I will make him into a great nation. But I will establish my covenant with Isaac, whom Sarah shall bear to you at this time next year' (Gen. 17:18-21).

Again:

> Be not displeased because of the boy [Ishmael] and because of your slave woman [Hagar]. Whatever Sarah says to you, do as she tells you, for through Isaac shall your offspring be named. And I will make a nation of the son of the slave woman also, because he is your offspring (Gen. 21:12-13).

In other words, there were to be two distinct lines of physical descent within the Abrahamic covenant; namely, through Ishmael and Isaac. The essential line would be through the younger, Isaac, not Ishmael. This much God had made clear to Abraham right from the earliest days of the covenant.

Again, as always, the New Testament must expound it all. And it most certainly does. Indeed, it adds to the revelation. This essential line of descent from Abraham through Isaac was continued, in turn, through only one of Isaac's twin sons; namely, Jacob (the younger, yet again), and not Esau. The New

Testament further explains that there is a spiritual meaning or dimension to this double line within the Abrahamic promise, a meaning of the utmost importance.[4] As Paul declared, within the Abrahamic covenant there have always been two sorts of Jews; that is, outward and inward, physical and spiritual:

> No one is a Jew who is merely one outwardly, nor is circumcision outward and physical. But a Jew is one inwardly, and circumcision is a matter of the heart, by the Spirit, not by the letter. His praise is not from man but from God (Rom. 2:28-29).

But it goes even deeper than this. The true descendants of Abraham, those in the Abrahamic covenant with whom God's eternal purpose has always been concerned, are not the physical descendants of the patriarch. No! God's eternal purpose has always been with the elect of all ages – those who will be brought to saving faith in Christ. This was, is, and always will be Abraham's spiritual seed:

> [Abraham] received the sign of circumcision as a seal of the righteousness that he had by faith while he was still uncircumcised. The purpose was to make him the father of all who believe without being circumcised, so that righteousness would be counted to them as well, and to make him the father of the circumcised who are not merely circumcised but who also walk in the footsteps of the faith that our father Abraham had before he was circumcised. For the promise to Abraham and his offspring that he would be heir of the world did not come through the law but through the righteousness of faith. For if it is the adherents of the law [of Moses] who are to be the heirs, faith is null and the promise is void. For the law brings wrath, but where there is no law there is no transgression. That is why it depends on faith, in order that the promise may rest on grace and be guaranteed to all his offspring – not only to the adherent of the law but also to the one who shares the faith of Abraham, who is the father of us all [that is, all believers] (Rom. 4:11-16).

As the apostle explained:

---

[4] See my *Infant* pp78-113.

The Mosaic Covenant

Immediately following his deliverance of Israel in the exodus from Egypt, 430 years after he had given Abraham his covenant, God, through Moses, gave the law to Israel, and only Israel, on Mount Sinai, thus distinguishing them as his national people under a covenant, a covenant that after Christ's death and resurrection would be known as the old covenant:

> And now, O Israel, listen to the statutes and the rules that I am teaching you, and do them, that you may live, and go in and take possession of the land that the LORD, the God of your fathers, is giving you. You shall not add to the word that I command you, nor take from it, that you may keep the commandments of the LORD your God that I command you... See, I have taught you statutes and rules, as the LORD my God commanded me, that you should do them in the land that you are entering to take possession of it. Keep them and do them, for that will be your wisdom and your understanding in the sight of the peoples, who, when they hear all these statutes, will say: 'Surely this great nation is a wise and understanding people'. For what great nation is there that has a god so near to it as the LORD our God is to us, whenever we call upon him? And what great nation is there, that has statutes and rules so righteous as all this law that I set before you today?...
>
> And Moses summoned all Israel and said to them: 'Hear, O Israel, the statutes and the rules that I speak in your hearing today, and you shall learn them and be careful to do them. The LORD our God made a covenant with us in Horeb. Not with our fathers did the LORD make this covenant, but with us, who are all of us here alive today...'...
>
> ...You are a people holy to the LORD your God. The LORD your God has chosen you to be a people for his treasured possession, out of all the peoples who are on the face of the earth. It was not because you were more in number than any other people that the LORD set his love on you and chose you, for you were the fewest of all peoples, but it is because the LORD loves you and is keeping the oath that he swore to your fathers, that the LORD has brought you out with a mighty hand and redeemed you from the house of slavery, from the hand of Pharaoh king of Egypt. Know therefore that the

LORD your God is God, the faithful God who keeps covenant and steadfast love with those who love him and keep his commandments, to a thousand generations, and repays to their face those who hate him, by destroying them. He will not be slack with one who hates him. He will repay him to his face. You shall therefore be careful to do the commandment and the statutes and the rules that I command you today. And because you listen to these rules and keep and do them, the LORD your God will keep with you the covenant and the steadfast love that he swore to your fathers... (Deut. 4:1 – 5:33; 7:8-12).

The psalmist made the same point:

[God] declares his word to Jacob, his statutes and rules to Israel. He has not dealt thus with any other nation; they do not know his rules (Ps. 147:19-20).

As did Paul:

Israelites... to them belong the adoption, the glory, the covenants, the giving of the law, the worship, and the promises (Rom. 9:4).

The Gentiles, it goes without saying, were not given the law. They were never under the Mosaic covenant. They were, and are, 'outside the law' (1 Cor. 9:21), 'alienated from the commonwealth of Israel and strangers to the covenants of promise,[1] having no hope and without God in the world' (Eph. 2:12). As Paul explained to the Romans, they are:

...without the law... For... Gentiles... do not have the law... they do not have the law (Rom. 2:12-14).

The children of Israel alone were under the Mosaic covenant, and this set them apart from all other people.

Now there was a striking – not to say, startling – contrast between the Mosaic and the Abrahamic covenants. While the Abrahamic covenant was a covenant of promise,[2] the Mosaic

---

[1] This general description includes the Mosaic covenant, of course, since Paul went on to speak of 'the dividing wall of hostility... the law of commandments expressed in ordinances' (Eph. 2:14-15).

[2] This is not to say there were no commands or punishments within that covenant. God issued the command to circumcise and warned that

The emphasised words prove it: the law was a works covenant. Now since all men in Adam are sinners, and all men are under law (whether Mosaic or pagan), and since all men are by nature dead in sins (Rom. 8:5-9), all men, therefore, are condemned and under the wrath of God (Eph. 2:1-3) under law (Rom. 2:12-15).

Paul, writing to the Romans, spelled it out, both for Israel under the law of Moses and for pagans under their own law:

For all who have sinned without the law will also perish without the law, and all who have sinned under the law will be judged by the law. For it is not the hearers of the law who are righteous before God, but the doers of the law who will be justified. For when Gentiles, who do not have the law, by nature do what the law requires, they are a law to themselves, even though they do not have the law. They show that the work of the law is written on their hearts, while their conscience also bears witness, and their conflicting thoughts accuse or even excuse them (Rom. 2:12-15).

The law brings wrath (Rom. 4:15).

The law... held us captive... Sin, seizing an opportunity through the commandment, produced in me all kinds of covetousness. For apart from the law, sin lies dead. I was once alive apart from the law, but when the commandment came, sin came alive and I died. The very commandment that promised life proved to be death to me. For sin, seizing an opportunity through the commandment, deceived me and through it killed me. So the law is holy, and the commandment is holy and righteous and good. Did that which is good, then, bring death to me? By no means! It was sin, producing death in me through what is good, in order that sin might be shown to be sin, and through the commandment might become sinful beyond measure (Rom. 7:6-13).

[The children of Israel,] being ignorant of the righteousness of God, and seeking to establish their own... did not submit to God's righteousness (Rom. 10:3).

As he did to the Corinthians:

The letter kills, but the Spirit gives life. Now if the ministry of death, carved in letters on stone, came with such glory that the

45

Israelites could not gaze at Moses' face because of its glory, which was being brought to an end, will not the ministry of the Spirit have even more glory? For if there was glory in the ministry of condemnation, the ministry of righteousness must far exceed it in glory. Indeed, in this case, what once had glory has come to have no glory at all, because of the glory that surpasses it. For if what was being brought to an end came with glory, much more will what is permanent have glory (2 Cor. 3:6-11).

James could not be clearer:

You are committing sin and are convicted by the law as transgressors. For whoever keeps the whole law but fails in one point has become accountable for all of it. For he who said: 'Do not commit adultery', also said: 'Do not murder'. If you do not commit adultery but do murder, you have become a transgressor of the law (Jas. 2:9-11).

Certain questions naturally and inevitably arise from all this:

What then shall we say? That the law is sin? (Rom. 7:7).

And this:

Why then the law?... Is the law then contrary to the promises of God? (Gal. 3:19-21).

The apostolic answers to such questions put the position beyond doubt:

Why then the law? It was added because of transgressions, until the offspring should come to whom the promise had been made, and it was put in place through angels by an intermediary... Is the law then contrary to the promises of God? Certainly not! For if a law had been given that could give life, then righteousness would indeed be by the law. But the Scripture imprisoned everything[8] under sin, so that the

---

[8] An interesting rendering of *ta panta*. Other versions have 'everyone', 'all'. Here it probably means 'all men'. Even so, through Christ, and under him, there will be a new heavens and a new earth (Rom. 8:18-22; 2 Pet. 3:13; see also Eph. 1:10,21-22; Col. 1:15-20). Ultimately, all will be to the glory of God (1 Cor. 15:20-28).

The Davidic Covenant

So great was the sense of the dignity that God had heaped upon him in forming a covenant with him, David could not help but rejoice:

> [God] has made with me an everlasting covenant, ordered in all things and secure (2 Sam. 23:5; see also 2 Sam. 7:8-16; 1 Chron. 17:7-14).

David simply could not get over the greatness of the privilege which had been afforded him. As he cried out to God in worship and prayer:

> Who am I, O Lord GOD, and what is my house, that you have brought me thus far? And yet this was a small thing in your eyes, O Lord GOD. You have spoken also of your servant's house for a great while to come, and this is instruction for mankind, O Lord GOD! And what more can David say to you? For you know your servant, O Lord GOD! Because of your promise, and according to your own heart, you have brought about all this greatness, to make your servant know it. Therefore you are great, O LORD God. For there is none like you, and there is no God besides you, according to all that we have heard with our ears. And who is like your people Israel, the one nation on earth whom God went to redeem to be his people, making himself a name and doing for them great and awesome things by driving out before your people, whom you redeemed for yourself from Egypt, a nation and its gods? And you established for yourself your people Israel to be your people forever. And you, O LORD, became their God. And now, O LORD God, confirm forever the word that you have spoken concerning your servant and concerning his house, and do as you have spoken. And your name will be magnified forever, saying: 'The LORD of hosts is God over Israel', and the house of your servant David will be established before you. For you, O LORD of hosts, the God of Israel, have made this revelation to your servant, saying: 'I will build you a house'. Therefore your servant has found courage to pray this prayer to you. And now, O Lord GOD, you are God, and your words are true, and you have promised this good thing to your

servant. Now therefore may it please you to bless the house of your servant, so that it may continue forever before you. For you, O Lord GOD, have spoken, and with your blessing shall the house of your servant be blessed forever (2 Sam. 7:18-29; see also 1 Chron. 17:16-27).

In all this, do not miss the 'everlasting'. Note the repeated 'forever' in God's declaration:

I have granted help to one who is mighty; I have exalted one chosen from the people. I have found David, my servant; with my holy oil I have anointed him, so that my hand shall be established with him; my arm also shall strengthen him. The enemy shall not outwit him; the wicked shall not humble him. I will crush his foes before him and strike down those who hate him. My faithfulness and my steadfast love shall be with him, and in my name shall his horn be exalted. I will set his hand on the sea and his right hand on the rivers. He shall cry to me: 'You are my Father, my God, and the Rock of my salvation'. And I will make him the firstborn, the highest of the kings of the earth. My steadfast love I will keep for him forever, and my covenant will stand firm for him. I will establish his offspring forever and his throne as the days of the heavens. If his children forsake my law and do not walk according to my rules, if they violate my statutes and do not keep my commandments, then I will punish their transgression with the rod and their iniquity with stripes, but I will not remove from him my steadfast love or be false to my faithfulness. I will not violate my covenant or alter the word that went forth from my lips. Once for all I have sworn by my holiness; I will not lie to David. His offspring shall endure forever, his throne as long as the sun before me. Like the moon it shall be established forever, a faithful witness in the skies (Ps. 89:19-37; see also Ps. 72).

Again:

The LORD swore to David a sure oath from which he will not turn back: 'One of the sons of your body I will set on your throne. If your sons keep my covenant and my testimonies that I shall teach them, their sons also forever shall sit on your throne'. For the LORD has chosen Zion; he has desired it for his dwelling place: 'This is my resting place forever; here I will dwell, for I have desired it. I will abundantly bless her

You [rightly] say that I am a king. For this purpose I was born and for this purpose I have come into the world – to bear witness to the truth (John 18:36-37).

In a last desperate throw, Pilate appealed to the Jews to release Jesus, arguing on the basis of his kingship, seeming not to realise that in taking this line he was actually waving the reddest of all rags before the Lord's accusers. In their rage by way of response, they even spoke of Caesar as their king! Spoke? I can hear the sneering, snarling tone – the contemptible tone – in their clash with the governor:

[Pilate] said to the Jews: 'Behold your King!' They cried out: 'Away with him, away with him, crucify him!' Pilate said to them: 'Shall I crucify your King?' The chief priests answered: 'We have no king but Caesar'. So he delivered him over to them to be crucified (John 19:14-16).

Again, after his resurrection, when commissioning his disciples, Christ declared:

All authority in heaven and on earth has been given to me. Go therefore and make disciples of all nations, baptising them in the name of the Father and of the Son and of the Holy Spirit, teaching them to observe all that I have commanded you. And behold, I am with you always, to the end of the age (Matt. 28:18-20).

Peter certainly proclaimed Christ as King, quoting Psalm 110 to support his words, arguing that David was a prophet:

Brothers, I may say to you with confidence about the patriarch David that he both died and was buried, and his tomb is with us to this day. Being therefore a prophet, and knowing that God had sworn with an oath to him that he would set one of his descendants on his throne, he foresaw and spoke about the resurrection of the Christ, that he was not abandoned to Hades, nor did his flesh see corruption. This Jesus God raised up, and of that we all are witnesses. Being therefore exalted at the right hand of God, and having received from the Father the promise of the Holy Spirit, he has poured out this that you yourselves are seeing and hearing. For David did not ascend into the heavens, but he himself says: 'The Lord said to my Lord: "Sit at my right hand, until I make your enemies your footstool'''. Let all the house of Israel therefore know for certain that God has made him both Lord and Christ, this Jesus whom you crucified (Acts 2:29-36).

The mob at Thessalonica accused Paul, Silas and other brothers of preaching Christ's kingship:

They are all acting against the decrees of Caesar, saying that there is another king, Jesus (Acts 17:7).

And Paul preached about Christ's descent from David when addressing the congregation in the synagogue at Antioch in Pisidia:

Of this man's offspring God has brought to Israel a Saviour, Jesus, as he promised... Those who live in Jerusalem and their rulers, because they did not recognise him nor understand the utterances of the prophets, which are read every sabbath, fulfilled them by condemning him (Acts 13:23,27).

And the apostle opened his letter to the Romans by referring to it:

Christ Jesus... who was descended from David according to the flesh and was declared to be the Son of God in power according to the Spirit of holiness by his resurrection from the dead, Jesus Christ our Lord (Rom. 1:1-4).

And, although the connection with David is absent when he expatiated on the matter to Timothy, Paul could not have been more emphatic on Christ's kingship:

Christ Jesus... in his testimony before Pontius Pilate made the good confession... our Lord Jesus Christ... he who is the blessed and only Sovereign, the King of kings and Lord of lords, who alone has immortality, who dwells in unapproachable light, whom no one has ever seen or can see. To him be honour and eternal dominion. Amen (1 Tim. 6:13-16).[5]

---

[5] The ESV ascribes this to Christ. Most versions, however, ascribe it to the Father. The literal Greek reads: 'Which in its own times shall show the blessed and only Ruler, the King of those being kings and Lord of those being lords...'.

I will take you from the nations and gather you from all the countries and bring you into your own land. I will sprinkle clean water on you, and you shall be clean from all your uncleannesses, and from all your idols I will cleanse you. And I will give you a new heart, and a new spirit I will put within you. And I will remove the heart of stone from your flesh and give you a heart of flesh. And I will put my Spirit within you, and cause you to walk in my statutes and be careful to obey my rules [just decrees or laws]. You shall dwell in the land that I gave to your fathers, and you shall be my people, and I will be your God. And I will deliver you from all your uncleannesses (Ezek. 36:24-28).

I will not hide my face any more from them, when I pour out my Spirit upon the house of Israel, declares the Lord GOD (Ezek. 39:29).

From the New Testament, we are left in no doubt about what the prophets were ultimately referring to when they spoke in this way.[4] They were speaking of the new covenant to be brought in by Christ, whose kingdom would embrace all the elect of all time, whether Jew or Gentile. In closing his letter to the Romans, Paul was explicit about the prophetic revelation in general, and its fulfilment in the new covenant:

Now to him who is able to strengthen you according to my gospel and the preaching of Jesus Christ, according to the revelation of the mystery that was kept secret for long ages but has now been disclosed and through the prophetic writings has been made known to all nations, according to the command of the eternal God, to bring about the obedience of faith – to the

---

[4] Of course, the pre-exilic passages were partially – but only very partially – fulfilled in the return of Israel after captivity, and the rebuilding of the (lesser) temple. What is more, the glorious prophetic passages (for example, Isa. 11), will only be completely realised in the eternal state, the new heavens and the new earth. No millennial Jewish kingdom, with Christ reigning in Jerusalem for 1000 years, which kingdom must be temporary and must end in disaster, can possibly account for the glorious promises of an eternal king reigning over an eternal kingdom, and doing so, without a break, from the time the prophets spoke.

only wise God be glory for evermore through Jesus Christ! Amen (Rom. 16:25-27).

As for the Isaiah 54 passage in particular, Christ had already set out its fulfilment:

> No one can come to me unless the Father who sent me draws him. And I will raise him up on the last day. It is written in the prophets: 'And they will all be taught by God'. Everyone who has heard and learned from the Father comes to me – not that anyone has seen the Father except he who is from God; he has seen the Father. Truly, truly, I say to you, whoever believes [in me] has eternal life (John 6:44-47).

As for the passage from Jeremiah, the writer to the Hebrews has told us, and told us at length and in explicit detail, how we should view it:

> Now if perfection had been attainable through the Levitical priesthood (for under it the people received the law), what further need would there have been for another priest to arise after the order of Melchizedek, rather than one named after the order of Aaron? For when there is a change in the priesthood, there is necessarily a change in the law as well... For on the one hand, a former commandment is set aside because of its weakness and uselessness (for the law made nothing perfect); but on the other hand, a better hope is introduced, through which we draw near to God... This makes Jesus the guarantor of a better covenant (Heb. 7:11-12,18-19,22).

> Christ has obtained a ministry that is as much more excellent than the old as the covenant he mediates is better, since it is enacted on better promises. For if that first covenant had been faultless, there would have been no occasion to look for a second. For he finds fault with them when he says: 'Behold, the days are coming, declares the Lord, when I will establish a new covenant with the house of Israel and with the house of Judah, not like the covenant that I made with their fathers on the day when I took them by the hand to bring them out of the land of Egypt. For they did not continue in my covenant, and so I showed no concern for them, declares the Lord. For this is the covenant that I will make with the house of Israel after those days, declares the Lord: I will put my laws into their minds, and write them on their hearts, and I will be their God,

alone (Rom. 4:1 – 5:21), this faith, following regeneration, leading immediately to the believer's union with Christ (Rom. 6:1-13). As a consequence, addressing believers, the apostle could say:

> Sin will have no dominion over you, since you are not under law but under grace. What then? Are we to sin because we are not under law but under grace? By no means! Do you not know that if you present yourselves to anyone as obedient slaves, you are slaves of the one whom you obey, either of sin, which leads to death, or of obedience, which leads to righteousness? But thanks be to God, that you who were once slaves of sin have become obedient from the heart to the standard of teaching to which you were committed, and, having been set free from sin, have become slaves of righteousness... But now that you have been set free from sin and have become slaves of God, the fruit you get leads to sanctification and its end, eternal life. For the wages of sin is death, but the free gift of God is eternal life in Christ Jesus our Lord (Rom. 6:14-23).

Again:

> My brothers, you also have died to the law through the body of Christ, so that you may belong to another, to him who has been raised from the dead, in order that we may bear fruit for God. For while we were living in the flesh, our sinful passions, aroused by the law, were at work in our members to bear fruit for death. But now we are released from the law, having died to that which held us captive, so that we serve in the new way of the Spirit and not in the old way of the written code (Rom. 7:4-6).[8]

And again:

> There is therefore now no condemnation for those who are in Christ Jesus. For the law of the Spirit of life has set you free in Christ Jesus from the law of sin and death. For God has done what the law, weakened by the flesh, could not do. By sending his own Son in the likeness of sinful flesh and for sin, he

---

[8] Just to point out that the 'law' in question is the law of Moses (or pagan law). Believers are under the law of Christ. The context makes this abundantly plain. See my *Believers*.

condemned sin in the flesh, in order that the righteous requirement of the law might be fulfilled in us, who walk not according to the flesh but according to the Spirit (Rom. 8:1-4).

And yet again:

Moses writes about the righteousness that is based on the law, that the person who does the commandments shall live by them. But the righteousness based on faith says... 'The word is near you, in your mouth and in your heart' (that is, the word of faith that we proclaim): That if you confess with your mouth that Jesus is Lord and believe in your heart that God raised him from the dead, you will be saved. For with the heart one believes and is justified, and with the mouth one confesses and is saved. For the Scripture says: 'Everyone who believes in him will not be put to shame'. For there is no distinction between Jew and Greek; for the same Lord is Lord of all, bestowing his riches on all who call on him. For 'everyone who calls on the name of the Lord will be saved' (Rom. 10:5-13).

He had made the very same points when writing to the Galatians:

Tell me, you who desire to be under the law, do you not listen to the law? For it is written that Abraham had two sons, one by a slave woman and one by a free woman. But the son of the slave was born according to the flesh, while the son of the free woman was born through promise. Now this may be interpreted allegorically: these women are two covenants. One is from Mount Sinai, bearing children for slavery; she is Hagar. Now Hagar is Mount Sinai in Arabia; she corresponds to the present Jerusalem, for she is in slavery with her children. But the Jerusalem above is free, and she is our mother. For it is written: 'Rejoice, O barren one who does not bear; break forth and cry aloud, you who are not in labour! For the children of the desolate one will be more than those of the one who has a husband'. Now you, brothers, like Isaac, are children of promise. But just as at that time he who was born according to the flesh persecuted him who was born according to the Spirit, so also it is now. But what does the Scripture say? 'Cast out the slave woman and her son, for the son of the slave woman shall not inherit with the son of the free woman'. So, brothers, we are not children of the slave but of the free

be born again". The wind blows where it wishes, and you hear its sound, but you do not know where it comes from or where it goes. So it is with everyone who is born of the Spirit' (John 3:3-8).

Paul expounded it in terms of the believer's union with Christ:

We were buried therefore with him by [spiritual] baptism[10] into death, in order that, just as Christ was raised from the dead by the glory of the Father, we too might walk in newness of life (Rom. 6:4).

And again:

Neither circumcision counts for anything, nor uncircumcision, but a new creation (Gal. 6:15).

Yet again:

Now this I say and testify in the Lord, that you must no longer walk as the Gentiles do, in the futility of their minds. They are darkened in their understanding, alienated from the life of God because of the ignorance that is in them, due to their hardness of heart. They have become callous and have given themselves up to sensuality, greedy to practice every kind of impurity. But that is not the way you learned Christ! – assuming that you have heard about him and were taught in him, as the truth is in Jesus, to put off your old self, which belongs to your former manner of life and is corrupt through deceitful desires, and to be renewed in the spirit of your minds, and to put on the new self, created after the likeness of God in true righteousness and holiness (Eph. 4:17-24).

Again:

You have put off the old self with its practices and have put on the new self, which is being renewed in knowledge after the image of its creator (Col. 3:9-10).

And it is all because of what the Father has accomplished through the work of Christ:

The Father... has qualified [us] to share in the inheritance of the saints in light. He has delivered us from the domain of

---

[10] For my reasons for this interpolation, see my *Baptist*.

darkness and transferred us to the kingdom of his beloved Son, in whom we have redemption, the forgiveness of sins (Col. 1:12-14).

Believers, therefore, are no longer dead in their sins, imprisoned in Adam, dragging out an existence in darkness.[11] Rather, they are alive in Christ, dwelling in light. And they can – and should – sing about it. William T.Matson certainly did:

> *Lord, I was blind: I could not see*
> *In thy marred visage any grace;*
> ***But now** the beauty of thy face*
> *In radiant vision dawns on me.*
>
> *Lord, I was deaf: I could not hear*
> *The thrilling music of thy voice;*
> ***But now** I hear thee and rejoice,*
> *And all thine uttered words are dear.*
>
> *Lord, I was dumb: I could not speak*
> *The grace and glory of thy Name;*
> ***But now**, as touched with living flame,*
> *My lips thine eager praises wake.*
> *Lord, I was dead: I could not stir*
> *My lifeless soul to come to thee;*
> ***But now**, since thou hast quickened me,*
> *I rise from sin's dark sepulchre.*
>
> *Lord, thou hast made the blind to see,*
> *The deaf to hear, the dumb to speak,*
> *The dead to live; and lo, I break*
> *The chains of my captivity.*

The scriptural 'but now', therefore, refers both to the change in epochs or ages – the old covenant giving way to the new – and to the individual conversion experience of every believer who, upon conversion, passes from death to life. Clearly there is an utter contrast between these two epochs, these two experiences.[12]

---

[11] I cannot call it 'living'.

[12] Some Reformed writers argue their case like this: the law was given to Israel to show them the way to live because they had been redeemed from Egypt. Similarly, since believers are redeemed from

John expressed it thus:

The law was given through Moses; grace and truth came through Jesus Christ (John 1:17).[13]

---

sin, they are, therefore, under that same law for sanctification. Is this right? Certainly not! The argument is fundamentally flawed, and patently so. Israel's redemption from Egypt by the passover typified the elect's redemption from sin by the blood of Christ, yes. Slavery in Egypt represented the dominion of sin, yes. The blood of the lamb represented the blood of Christ, yes. Canaan represented the rest which the redeemed enjoy in Christ, yes. (But this is not to be limited to heaven. Nor is it to be transferred to the keeping the first day of the week – for which there is not the slightest biblical warrant. Matt. 11:28-30 is the rest in question). But what in the new covenant corresponds to the giving of the law by Moses on Sinai? The believer, like Israel, has had his exodus from his Egypt. He too has come to a mountain and received a law. He too is in a covenant. And he too has entered his promised land. But his exodus is a *new* exodus, he has come to a *new* mountain, he has been put into a *new* covenant, and entered a *new* realm. The two covenants and two sets of events are chalk and cheese. They must not be cobbled together. To find 'spiritual equivalents' for Egypt, the exodus, the mountains and the passover, *but not the law*, is at best inconsistent. Yet this is the very thing that many do. While they rightly speak of the blood of Christ 'replacing' the passover, redemption from sin 'replacing' deliverance from Egypt, and so on, they nevertheless try to argue the law of Sinai passes over virtually unchanged into the new covenant. It will not do. Something has 'replaced' the giving of the law to Israel through Moses, just as the realm of sin is the spiritual equivalent of Egypt, the realm of grace is the spiritual Canaan, and the blood of Christ has fulfilled the typical blood of the passover lamb. Reformed writers like to find a spiritual equivalent for one part of a passage or an episode (the exodus, as above, or Jeremiah 31, or the rules for circumcision, for instance) but not the other. I say it again. It will not do! What is more, the 'new' must be stressed. The old covenant was a shadow; the new, the reality. These two covenants must not be muddled up. In particular, the law of the new covenant is not the law of the old. See my *Christ* pp67-68.

[13] Note the missing 'but'. For the importance of this, see Appendix 3. See also Rom. 4:15; 6:14; 7:4-6; 10:5ff; 2 Cor. 3:6-11; 3:1-10 and so on.

And one of the great contrasts between the old and new covenants is that the old covenant (a covenant of shadow) gives way to the new covenant (a covenant of substance) – the promise is fulfilled. In my dinner-table illustration, we should now put away the menu, lift our knife and fork, square our elbows, and start to partake of the meal and enjoy it. There is, however, just a little more to say about the menu. And that is what the following chapter is all about.

later, but Christ is faithful over God's house as a son (Heb. 3:1-6).

Exodus

Take the exodus of the children of Israel from Egypt under Moses. In redeeming Israel from Egyptian slavery, God gave Israel the passover (Exodus 12), then the sabbath (Exodus 16), then the law at Sinai (Exodus 20 and on), and then, following a generation of judgement in the wilderness because of the people's refusal to trust God and enter the promised land at once, took them into Canaan under Joshua. All these shadows have given way to the reality. Believers, through faith in Christ, by his sacrifice, have been delivered from the bondage of sin, death and law, united to Christ, brought into rest, given the law of Christ, and will be brought into eternal glory. To list scriptures at this point would be invidious – read the entirety of the post-Pentecost Scriptures and see!

Sabbath

The new-covenant sabbath is Christ (Heb. 3:7 – 4:11); he gives rest to his people:

> Come to me, all who labour and are heavy laden, and I will give you rest. Take my yoke upon you, and learn from me, for I am gentle and lowly in heart, and you will find rest for your souls. For my yoke is easy, and my burden is light (Matt. 11:28-30).

And:

> Therefore, since we have been justified by faith, we have peace with God through our Lord Jesus Christ. Through him we have also obtained access by faith into this grace in which we stand, and we rejoice in hope of the glory of God (Rom. 5:1-2).

As the writer to the Hebrews put it, speaking of the believers' present experience of Christ – present experience, I stress – culminating in the eternal rest they will enjoy in glory:

There remains a sabbath rest for the people of God, for whoever has entered God's rest has also rested from his works as God did from his (Heb. 4:9-10).[8]

Priesthood

The great high priest of the new covenant is Christ:

We have a great high priest who has passed through the heavens, Jesus, the Son of God... being designated by God a high priest after the order of Melchizedek... The Lord has sworn and will not change his mind: 'You are a priest forever'. This makes Jesus the guarantor of a better covenant... The law appoints men in their weakness as high priests, but the word of the oath, which came later than the law, appoints a Son who has been made perfect forever... The point in what we are saying is this: we have such a high priest, one who is seated at the right hand of the throne of the Majesty in heaven, a minister in the holy places, in the true tent that the Lord set up, not man... Christ appeared as a high priest of the good things that have come, then through the greater and more perfect tent (not made with hands, that is, not of this creation) he entered once for all into the holy places, not by means of the blood of goats and calves but by means of his own blood, thus securing an eternal redemption... Therefore he is the mediator of a new covenant (Heb. 4:15 – 5:10; 7:1 – 8:2; 9:11-15).[9]

Sacrifice

The sacrifice of the new covenant – the one and only effective sacrifice for all time – is that of Christ:

He entered once for all into the holy places, not by means of the blood of goats and calves but by means of his own blood, thus securing an eternal redemption. If the blood of goats and bulls, and the sprinkling of defiled persons with the ashes of a heifer, sanctify for the purification of the flesh, how much more will the blood of Christ, who through the eternal Spirit offered himself without blemish to God, purify our conscience from dead works to serve the living God. Therefore he is the mediator of a new covenant... He has appeared once for all at

---

[8] See my *Essential*.
[9] And, of course, all believers are priests. See my *The Priesthood*.

But you will receive power when the Holy Spirit has come upon you, and you will be my witnesses in Jerusalem and in all Judea and Samaria, and to the end of the earth (Acts 1:8).

The conclusion?: 'Men of Galilee, why do you stand looking into heaven?' (Acts 1:11). If I may accommodate the words: 'Believer, stop wasting your time, wondering about some earthly Davidic kingdom, engaging in such speculations.[17] Get on with preaching the gospel throughout the world!'

And it is the very way in which Peter, for example, went on. In his ensuing ministry, he never stopped referring to the prophets, but never once did he do so to talk of an earthly kingdom. He always spoke of the gospel and the present (and eternal future) glories of the gospel for believers (Acts 3:18-24; 10:42-43; 1 Pet. 1:10-12, for instance).

In short, there is no support of any millennial kingdom in this passage. The land promise is not fulfilled in that way.

So, what, in the new covenant with and for the Israel of God (Gal. 6:16), is the spiritual fulfilment of this land promise? The key lies in the word 'rest'. The land promise represented 'rest' for Israel. 'Rest' was always the essence of the promise. Entering the land, settlement in the land, was entering rest. And it is the new Israel, and only the new Israel, which truly experiences that rest. The writer to the Hebrews explained:

Therefore, as the Holy Spirit says: 'Today, if you hear his voice, do not harden your hearts as in the rebellion, on the day of testing in the wilderness, where your fathers put me to the test and saw my works for forty years. Therefore I was provoked with that generation, and said: "They always go astray in their heart; they have not known my ways". As I swore in my wrath: "They shall not enter my rest"'. Take care, brothers, lest there be in any of you an evil, unbelieving heart, leading you to fall away from the living God. But exhort one another every day, as long as it is called 'today', that none of you may be hardened by the deceitfulness of sin. For we have

---

[17] Not a few in my experience do more than *engage* in such. Once bitten by the bug, they are consumed with Israel and the coming kingdom. It is tragic. And the consequences can be very severe indeed.

87

come to share in Christ, if indeed we hold our original confidence firm to the end. As it is said: 'Today, if you hear his voice, do not harden your hearts as in the rebellion'. For who were those who heard and yet rebelled? Was it not all those who left Egypt led by Moses? And with whom was he provoked for forty years? Was it not with those who sinned, whose bodies fell in the wilderness? And to whom did he swear that they would not enter his rest, but to those who were disobedient? So we see that they were unable to enter because of unbelief.[18]

Therefore, while the promise of entering his rest still stands, let us fear lest any of you should seem to have failed to reach it. For good news came to us just as to them, but the message they heard did not benefit them, because they were not united by faith with those who listened. For we who have believed enter that rest, as he has said: 'As I swore in my wrath: "They shall not enter my rest"', although his works were finished from the foundation of the world. For he has somewhere spoken of the seventh day in this way: 'And God rested on the seventh day from all his works'. And again in this passage he said: 'They shall not enter my rest'. Since therefore it remains for some to enter it, and those who formerly received the good news failed to enter because of disobedience, again he appoints a certain day: 'Today', saying through David so long afterward, in the words already quoted: 'Today, if you hear his voice, do not harden your hearts'. For if Joshua had given them rest, God would not have spoken of another day later on. So then, there remains a sabbath rest for the people of God, for whoever has entered God's rest has also rested from his works as God did from his. Let us therefore strive to enter that rest, so that no one may fall by the same sort of disobedience (Heb. 3:7 – 4:11).[19]

The deliverance of Israel from Egypt and the bringing of Israel into the land of promise was a shadow or picture of the sinner passing from death to life, being taken out of Adam and being brought into Christ (Col. 1:13). But the shadow, as the meaning of the words used indicate, was blurred. While there was a gap

---

[18] Unable to enter the land and, as he had just said, and kept saying, unable to enter rest.

[19] Thus Paul can quote the fifth commandment with its land promise when writing to believers (Eph. 6:1-6; Deut. 5:16).

reproach of Christ greater wealth than the treasures of Egypt, for he was looking to the reward' (Heb. 11:26). Christ, not Canaan![21]

No wonder then that the writer of the letter of the Hebrews, in closing this mighty eleventh chapter, and linking all the true descendants of Abraham – that is, all believers down all the years, both before and after the coming of Christ – spoke thus:

> And all these, though commended through their faith, did not receive what was promised, since God had provided something better for us, that apart from us they should not be made perfect (Heb. 11:39-40).

And as he later said, addressing all true believers living in the days of the new covenant:

> You have come to Mount Zion and to the city of the living God, the heavenly Jerusalem, and to innumerable angels in festal gathering, and to the assembly of the firstborn who are enrolled in heaven, and to God, the judge of all, and to the spirits of the righteous made perfect, and to Jesus, the mediator of a new covenant, and to the sprinkled blood that speaks a better word than the blood of Abel (Heb. 12:22-24).

Paul, contrasting the physical and the spiritual Jerusalems, could not put it more plainly:

> The present Jerusalem... is in slavery with her children. But the Jerusalem above is free, and she is our mother (Gal. 4:25-26).

In light of all this, it is nothing short of tragic to find believers thinking about the Abrahamic land-promise in terms of Canaan and an earthly Jewish kingdom. As even those who hold to a millennial kingdom under Christ have to admit, that kingdom – allowing its existence, for sake of argument – will end in ruins. The Abrahamic promise, however, is fulfilled, and has always been certain to be fulfilled, in a kingdom that has foundations

---

[21] True, it was a grievous disappointment to him that, because of his sin, he was not allowed to enter the land but see it only from a distance (Deut. 3:23-27; 34:1-4). Even so, his eye was firmly fixed by faith on Christ.

that will never crumble – a city, a kingdom that will never disappear. The land promise has always pointed to Christ and the everlasting rest to be enjoyed by all who are united by faith to him. That rest begins for all believers immediately at conversion, and will culminate in the eternal glory to come in the new heavens and the new earth. *This* is the climax of the new covenant:

> Blessed be the God and Father of our Lord Jesus Christ! According to his great mercy, he has caused us to be born again to a living hope through the resurrection of Jesus Christ from the dead, to an inheritance that is imperishable, undefiled, and unfading, kept in heaven for you, who by God's power are being guarded through faith for a salvation ready to be revealed in the last time. In this you rejoice... (1 Pet. 1:3-6).

> According to [God's] promise we are waiting for new heavens and a new earth in which righteousness dwells (2 Pet. 3:13; see also Rom. 8:21; Rev. 21:1).

Summary

The old covenant played a vital role in the covenant history of redemption, not least to foreshadow the glories of Christ in the new covenant. And this it did, as God always intended. Clearly, then, Christ, when he died and rose again and poured out his Spirit, brought the old covenant with all its shadows to its God-ordained end by establishing the new covenant. The fulfilment of the shadows meant that they had gone, and gone for good; the substance had come, and come permanently. The final realisation of the shadows in all their fullness, of course will only come about in the eternal state of glory, which will be ushered in, at God's appointed time, at the return of Christ. Nevertheless, we must not minimise the believer's wealth in Christ even now. Nor must we diminish it by trying to cling on to any old-covenant shadow, whether temple (tabernacle), sabbath, altar, sacrifice, a priestly class, and the like. All are gone in Christ, swallowed up and rendered obsolete in him and yet the believer has them all – spiritually speaking – in his Redeemer.

And that, apart from spelling out the practical consequences of this change of covenant for us today, should signal the end to this look into the history of redemption through covenants. Alas, it does not...

Paul Against the Law Men

Why did Paul write in the following way to the Galatians? Bear in mind that the Galatian churches, to whom the apostle was writing, were made up mainly of Gentiles:

> It is written that Abraham had two sons, one by a slave woman and one by a free woman. But the son of the slave was born according to the flesh, while the son of the free woman was born through promise. Now this may be interpreted allegorically: these women are two covenants. One is from Mount Sinai, bearing children for slavery; she is Hagar. Now Hagar is Mount Sinai in Arabia; she corresponds to the present Jerusalem, for she is in slavery with her children. But the Jerusalem above is free, and she is our mother. For it is written: 'Rejoice, O barren one who does not bear; break forth and cry aloud, you who are not in labour! For the children of the desolate one will be more than those of the one who has a husband'. Now you, brothers, like Isaac, are children of promise. But just as at that time he who was born according to the flesh persecuted him who was born according to the Spirit, so also it is now. But what does the Scripture say? 'Cast out the slave woman and her son, for the son of the slave woman shall not inherit with the son of the free woman'. So, brothers, we are not children of the slave but of the free woman. For freedom Christ has set us free; stand firm therefore, and do not submit again to a yoke of slavery (Gal. 4:21 – 5:1).

This was not the only time that Paul wrote in such a way, even in the same letter. Indeed, beginning at Galatians 2:1, he never left the theme throughout his letter.[1] And this was not the only church or churches (comprised mainly of Gentiles) to whom he wrote in a similar vein. Take his letter to the Philippians. The apostle could not have been more blunt:

> Look out for the dogs, look out for the evildoers, look out for those who mutilate the flesh. For we are the circumcision, who worship by the Spirit of God and glory in Christ Jesus and put

---

[1] And, with hindsight, we know he was referring to the same matter from Gal. 1:6 and on.

no confidence in the flesh – though I myself have reason for confidence in the flesh also. If anyone else thinks he has reason for confidence in the flesh, I have more: circumcised on the eighth day, of the people of Israel, of the tribe of Benjamin, a Hebrew of Hebrews; as to the law, a Pharisee; as to zeal, a persecutor of the church; as to righteousness under the law, blameless. But whatever gain I had, I counted as loss for the sake of Christ. Indeed, I count everything as loss because of the surpassing worth of knowing Christ Jesus my Lord. For his sake I have suffered the loss of all things and count them as rubbish, in order that I may gain Christ and be found in him, not having a righteousness of my own that comes from the law, but that which comes through faith in Christ, the righteousness from God that depends on faith – that I may know him and the power of his resurrection, and may share his sufferings, becoming like him in his death, that by any means possible I may attain the resurrection from the dead (Phil. 3:2-11).

As he wrote to the Colossians:

As you received Christ Jesus the Lord, so walk in him, rooted and built up in him and established in the faith, just as you were taught, abounding in thanksgiving. See to it that no one takes you captive by philosophy and empty deceit, according to human tradition, according to the elemental spirits of the world, and not according to Christ. For in him the whole fullness of deity dwells bodily, and you have been filled in him, who is the head of all rule and authority. In him also you were circumcised with a circumcision made without hands, by putting off the body of the flesh, by the circumcision of Christ, having been buried with him in baptism, in which you were also raised with him through faith in the powerful working of God, who raised him from the dead. And you, who were dead in your trespasses and the uncircumcision of your flesh, God made alive together with him, having forgiven us all our trespasses, by cancelling the record of debt that stood against us with its legal demands. This he set aside, nailing it to the cross. He disarmed the rulers and authorities and put them to open shame, by triumphing over them in him. Therefore let no one pass judgement on you in questions of food and drink, or with regard to a festival or a new moon or a sabbath. These are a shadow of the things to come, but the substance belongs to Christ. Let no one disqualify you, insisting on asceticism and worship of angels, going on in detail about visions, puffed up without reason by his sensuous mind, and not holding fast to the Head, from whom the whole body, nourished and knit together through its joints and ligaments, grows with a growth that is from God. If with Christ you died to the elemental spirits of the world, why, as if you were still alive in the world, do you submit to regulations – 'Do not handle, Do not taste, Do not touch' (referring to things that all perish as they are used) – according to human precepts and teachings? These have indeed an appearance of wisdom in promoting self-made religion and asceticism and severity to the body, but they are of no value in stopping the indulgence of the flesh.

If then you have been raised with Christ, seek the things that are above, where Christ is, seated at the right hand of God. Set your minds on things that are above, not on things that are on earth. For you have died, and your life is hidden with Christ in God. When Christ who is your life appears, then you also will appear with him in glory. Put to death therefore what is earthly in you: sexual immorality, impurity, passion, evil desire, and covetousness, which is idolatry. On account of these the wrath of God is coming. In these you too once walked, when you were living in them. But now you must put them all away: anger, wrath, malice, slander, and obscene talk from your mouth. Do not lie to one another, seeing that you have put off the old self with its practices and have put on the new self, which is being renewed in knowledge after the image of its creator. Here there is not Greek and Jew, circumcised and uncircumcised, barbarian, Scythian, slave, free; but Christ is all, and in all (Col. 2:6 – 3:11).[2]

So why did Paul write so much, and so often, and in such detail, about the law, and do so to Gentiles? Why did he write, to largely Gentile readers, such extended passages as Romans 3:19 – 4:25 and 6:14 – 8:4, not forgetting Romans 10:4-6? And why did he write 2 Corinthians 3:6-18? All these passages were written to churches that (almost certainly) had a large Gentile constituency. So why bother to tell Gentiles so much about the law? And why do it with such passion and in such detail? The Gentiles never were under the law of Moses (Rom. 2:14; 1 Cor.

---

[2] Yes, some of this is to do with pagan laws, but not all of it. Note the clear references to circumcision, sabbath *etc.*

9:21; Gal. 2:3,14) since that law had been given solely to Israel (Deut. 4:5-8; Ps. 147:19-20; Rom. 9:4). So, I ask again, why did Paul write so much and so often to Gentiles about a law they were never under?

We do not have to guess. Take the case of the Galatians. The alarming truth is, the Galatians were seriously considering putting themselves under the law. And this is why Paul demanded of them: 'Tell me, you who desire to be under the law, do you not listen to the law? For it is written...' (Gal. 4:21). The Galatian churches were being bitten with a 'desire to be under the law', thus 'deserting him who called you in the grace of Christ and [were] turning to a different gospel', the very thought of which brought the apostle's: 'I am astonished that you are so quickly deserting him who called you in the grace of Christ and are turning to a different gospel – not that there is another one' (Gal. 1:6-7).

Where had this desire come from, this desire to be under the law? Why did Gentile believers want to go under a fulfilled and obsolete covenant (Heb. 8:13), a covenant that was never theirs but had been expressly given to the Jews, and only them? Why? Because, as I will explain, certain teachers – Judaisers – had infiltrated the churches, including those in Galatia, and were arguing that Gentile believers (believers, especially *Gentile* believers, I stress) – needed to come under the law of Moses, and this for their progressive sanctification. The full extract just quoted sets the scene:

> I am astonished that you are so quickly deserting him who called you in the grace of Christ and are turning to a different gospel – not that there is another one, but there are some who trouble you and want to distort the gospel of Christ (Gal. 1:6-7).

The law men, however, had opened their campaign by travelling from Jerusalem to Antioch in Syria. As Luke put it:

Nor was this problem confined to Galatia. You can't fail to sense – or, at least, I hope you can't fail to sense – how much muscle Paul was flexing here. Although I have already quoted his words, they bear repeating:

> Look out for the dogs, look out for the evildoers, look out for those who mutilate the flesh. For we are the circumcision, who worship by the Spirit of God and glory in Christ Jesus and put no confidence in the flesh – though I myself have reason for confidence in the flesh also. If anyone else thinks he has reason for confidence in the flesh, I have more: circumcised on the eighth day, of the people of Israel, of the tribe of Benjamin, a Hebrew of Hebrews; as to the law, a Pharisee; as to zeal, a persecutor of the church; as to righteousness under the law, blameless. But whatever gain I had, I counted as loss for the sake of Christ. Indeed, I count everything as loss because of the surpassing worth of knowing Christ Jesus my Lord. For his sake I have suffered the loss of all things and count them as rubbish, in order that I may gain Christ and be found in him, not having a righteousness of my own that comes from the law, but that which comes through faith in Christ, the righteousness from God that depends on faith – that I may know him and the power of his resurrection, and may share his sufferings, becoming like him in his death, that by any means possible I may attain the resurrection from the dead (Phil. 3:2-11).

Strong stuff! A spade's a spade here all right!

Herein lies the reason for the apostle writing so much and so vehemently upon the law. His pastoral heart for Christ's people, and his determination to uphold the gospel at all costs, drove him on. As we have seen, the issue had erupted at Antioch. But the truth is, these law men were attacking nearly all the churches of the New Testament. They were infiltrating themselves – sneaking – into all the New Testament churches. This is how they had gone about their work among the Galatian churches, and how the apostle reacted to it:

> I [Paul] went up again to Jerusalem with Barnabas, taking Titus along with me. I went up because of a revelation and set before them (though privately before those who seemed influential) the gospel that I proclaim among the Gentiles, in order to make sure I was not running or had not run in vain.

But even Titus, who was with me, was not forced to be circumcised, though he was a Greek. Yet because of false brothers *secretly brought in* – who slipped in to spy out our freedom that we have in Christ Jesus, so that they might bring us into slavery – to them we did not yield in submission even for a moment, so that the truth of the gospel might be preserved for you. And from those who seemed to be influential (what they were makes no difference to me; God shows no partiality) – those, I say, who seemed influential added nothing to me. On the contrary, when they saw that I had been entrusted with the gospel to the uncircumcised, just as Peter had been entrusted with the gospel to the circumcised (for he who worked through Peter for his apostolic ministry to the circumcised worked also through me for mine to the Gentiles), and when James and Cephas and John, who seemed to be pillars, perceived the grace that was given to me, they gave the right hand of fellowship to Barnabas and me, that we should go to the Gentiles and they to the circumcised. Only, they asked us to remember the poor, the very thing I was eager to do. But when Cephas came to Antioch, I opposed him to his face, because he stood condemned. For before certain men came from James, he was eating with the Gentiles; but when they came he drew back and separated himself, fearing the circumcision party. And the rest of the Jews acted hypocritically along with him, so that even Barnabas was led astray by their hypocrisy. But when I saw that their conduct was not in step with the truth of the gospel, I said to Cephas before them all: 'If you, though a Jew, live like a Gentile and not like a Jew, how can you force the Gentiles to live like Jews?' (Gal. 2:1-14).

Paul was not alone. Jude tackled a similar issue brought about by infiltrators:

Beloved, although I was very eager to write to you about our common salvation, I found it necessary to write appealing to you to contend for the faith that was once for all delivered to the saints. For certain people *have crept in unnoticed* who long ago were designated for this condemnation, ungodly people, who pervert the grace of our God into sensuality and deny our only Master and Lord, Jesus Christ (Jude 3-4).

The law men were, in effect, trying to reverse the covenant history of redemption by taking new-covenant men and women back under the old covenant. And Paul would not tolerate it for a moment! What! Allow these infiltrators – these law men – to try to undo the history of redemption through covenants? Allow them to try to drag saints back under the old covenant, now that it has been fulfilled by Christ and rendered obsolete, he having fulfilled its God-ordained purpose in the unfolding history of redemption to a lost world? Allow the law men to try, in effect, to undo or thwart God's eternal purpose? Never! The apostle, whatever it cost him, would not yield – no, not for a moment. And *that* shows how important the history of redemption through covenants is. Nothing, nothing, must be allowed to undo it.

Now, as we know, there is nothing new under the sun (Eccles. 1:9). As I have repeatedly shown in many of my works, this law pressure is still being applied today, and as strongly as ever. John Calvin, with his threefold use of the law – especially with his view that the law is a whip to beat lazy asses (he is talking about believers, remember!) into progressive sanctification – set the thing in concrete. His doctrine was taken up and fine-tuned by the Puritans, and has become received wisdom (whether knowingly or unknowingly) ever since. As a consequence, legal preaching – with all its concomitants and consequences – is far more common today than gospel preaching. And, as far as law preaching takes hold, to that extent it unravels God's history of redemption through covenants. And it is not just a question of history! The teaching of law men today, every bit as much as in the days of the apostles, spells bondage for believers, to say nothing of the damage it inflicts on unbelievers. These are matters of the highest concern. I urge all believers to weigh the apostle's words to the Galatians, and act upon them:

> Brothers, we are not children of the slave but of the free woman. For freedom Christ has set us free; stand firm therefore, and do not submit again to a yoke of slavery (Gal. 4:31 – 5:1).

Brothers and sisters, we are not under the law of Moses. We are under the law of Christ.[10] And so to the concluding chapter...

---

[10] Do not miss the wordplay on 'yoke' in Matt. 11:29-30; Acts 15:10; Gal. 5:1).

Application

At this stage in the Olive Branch Conference, with one session to go, I wanted to do two things; that is, I knew I had to attempt the difficult, if not impossible, task of riding two horses at once. First, I wanted to bring the conference to a suitable conclusion, in order to round off the three or four days we had spent together. But I also wanted to preach the gospel and make pointed application of all that we had thought about in those days. I attempted the impossible by preaching on Colossians 3:11: 'Christ is all'.

William Perkins, the Puritan who was so influential in setting the mark for fellow-Puritans to reach as regards preaching, had an excellent dictum: 'What's the use of it?', he would ask. In my dinner-table illustration, it is all very well laying the table and bringing in the meal, but...! Imagine it! Guests sitting round a table, a table well and truly laid, with the meal spread before them, and all they can do is discuss what is before them – concentrating on the vitamins, the enzymes, the antioxidants... the balance of carbohydrates, proteins and fats, the number of calories and the amount of cholesterol in the food. All they can talk about is the presentation of the dishes, asking for the recipes! Discuss, debate, admire... is that what it's all about? Surely not! The meal is meant to be eaten, digested, enjoyed! Above all, the meal is to give the diners power and energy to sustain and encourage life and work. This, after all, is God's purpose in creating the raw material, the cook's purpose in preparing the food, and the ultimate end of our sitting at the table. Applying the illustration, what's the use of the history of redemption through covenants? What practical use, that is.

That is what I tried to address at Olive Branch. In this closing chapter of this book, however, I will confine myself to a summary of the sort of application that should be made of all we have looked at.[1] I direct my remarks to both the unbeliever and the believer.

We have been thinking about the covenant history of redemption. Redemption. Salvation, deliverance, being set free. Set free from what? From sin, its condemnation, guilt, power and, ultimately, its presence; set free from bondage, slavery, God's wrath, death and law.[2]

Very well. Reader, are you redeemed? Can you speak of Christ in this way: 'The Son of God... loved me and gave himself for me' (Gal. 2:20)? Do you know that Christ has redeemed you? Do you feel it? In other words, are *you* trusting Christ for *your* salvation and submitting to him as *your* Lord?

Redemption history through covenants. Very well. Reader, where are you in this history? Which covenant are you in? You most certainly are in one covenant or another – whether or not you realise or acknowledge the fact. Which law are you under? You are under one law or another, spiritually speaking. Which? Whose? Who is your husband – Christ or the law (Rom. 7:4-6)? Which mountain are you living on (Heb. 12:18-24)? And you most certainly are living on one of two mountains – spiritually speaking – whether or not you recognise or like to admit it.[3] And if you are not living on Mount Zion, then you *are* living on Mount Sinai – and that means you are vainly hoping to be right with God through your works. Give it up at once! Trust Christ,

---

[1] Those who wish to hear what I actually said can use the video and audio links already given. In addition, there are the last two sessions of the conference I addressed in Sacramento in February 2016: http://www.sermonaudio.com/search.asp?seriesOnly=true&currSectio n=sermonstopic&sourceid=ncbcnorcal&keyword=Evangelism+In+Th e+New+Covenant&keyworddesc=Evangelism+In+The+New+Covena nt

[2] But believers are, of course, under Christ's law.

[3] While the law of Moses, given on Sinai, belonged only to Israel, nevertheless, as I have explained, in Scripture, Israel is treated as a paradigm to address Gentiles who, even though they are not under the law of Moses, are under their own law.

and rest yourself in his finished work! As the writer to the Hebrews put it:

> See that you do not refuse him who is speaking. For if they did not escape when they refused him who warned them on earth, much less will we escape if we reject him who warns from heaven... for our God is a consuming fire (Heb. 12:25,29).[4]

And then, of course, there is the believer. What are the consequences of this history of redemption through covenants for you as a believer? Well, as a believer, you are not under the law of Moses, certainly, but you most definitely are under the law of Christ in the new covenant. And this has huge ramifications for your assurance, progressive sanctification and perseverance unto eternal glorification. I would love to develop all these matters here, but since I have done so at length elsewhere,[5] I leave it there.[6]

---

[4] Those words were written to professing believers who were thinking of going back from Christ. How much more, then, do they apply to you, if you are an unbeliever!

[5] See my *Assurance*; *Fivefold*; *Positional*; *Believers*.

6 The previously-quoted reader of my mss made a comment with which I so much agree. I quote her because, having written as firmly as I have on believers under the law of Christ, under the written word, I have also argued, equally firmly, that this does not mean 'recipe preaching', 'penny-in-the slot preaching', mere conformity to rules, and I am delighted to quote my (American) friend's way of putting it: 'I think people, and preachers most of all, do not like freedom as much as they say they do! They prefer cut and dried rules, a checklist, a protocol to (outwardly) live by and, in the case of leaders, to measure how the flock is doing. Much easier than getting down to the nitty-gritty of how that ole walk with Jesus is actually going! In short, things just seem a little too loosey-goosey [that is, relaxed] under the doctrine of grace – you know, as you started this book, there's a point here where each person has to figure this out on his own before the throne. And... how can you order and run an organisation [the church as an institution] with that – isn't that every man doing what is right in his own eyes, blah blah blah *ad nauseam*?[!] I believe this is what drives a LOT of wrong doctrine – the understandable, but yet pitiful fear of being free, and therefore personally responsible, to serve the Lord in spirit and in truth'.

The history of redemption through covenants is not simply an academic discussion. I did not treat it as such at Olive Branch, nor did the friends arrange the conference simply to have discussion about the covenants and redemption. Issues of life and death hang upon it. Eternal consequences hang upon it. And all of it in a highly personal way. In saying this I am addressing all believers, including myself. But I am also addressing unbelievers. Do not rest until you know you are redeemed by Christ and in the new covenant, and then live the rest of your days increasing in the experiential joy of this truth, to the glory of God, in Christ, by the Holy Spirit.

APPENDICES

fulfilled the obedience in which Adam failed... but it would not be correct to say, however, that Christ's obedience was the same in content or demand. Christ was called on to obey in radically different conditions, and required to fulfil radically different demands. Christ was a sin-bearer and the climactic demand was [for him] to die. This was not true of Adam. Christ came to redeem; not so Adam. So Christ rendered the whole-souled totality [of?] obedience in which Adam failed, but under totally different conditions and with incomparably greater demands.

Unfortunately, Murray thought 'the Mosaic covenant was distinctly redemptive in character and was continuous with and extensive of [as?] the Abrahamic covenants'.[14]

What about this for arguing black is white? Witsius thought Adam was under the covenant of works which 'in substance [corresponded] with what is expressed in the ten commandments'. After Adam fell, God instituted a 'new covenant of grace' with him. Witsius based this on the fact that when God says 'new, he makes the first old' (Heb. 8:13). 'It is indeed true, that the [writer], in that place, does not speak precisely of the covenant of works, but of the old economy of the covenant of grace... Yet we properly build on his [that is, the writer to the Hebrews as interpreted by Witsius] reasoning'.[15] I do not apologise for the word – Hermann Witsius was a great man, I have no doubt – but this is rubbish!

---

[14] John Murray: *The Adamic Administration*, in *Collected Writings of John Murray, Volume 2: Systematic Theology*, The Banner of Truth Trust, Edinburgh, 1977, pp49-50,58.
[15] Zens pp24-25,92-93, quoting Witsius.

Appendix 2
Three Verses Misunderstood

I refer to Galatians 3:23-25, the climax of Galatians 3:10-25. I quote the verses:

> Before faith came, we were kept under guard by the law, kept [literally 'confined' – footnote] for the faith which would afterwards be revealed. Therefore the law was our tutor to bring us to Christ, that we might be justified by faith. But after faith has come, we are no longer under a tutor (NKJV).

And in other versions:

> Before faith came, we were kept under the law, shut up unto the faith which should afterwards be revealed. Wherefore the law was our schoolmaster to bring us unto Christ, that we might be justified by faith. But after that faith is come, we are no longer under a schoolmaster (AV).

> Before faith came, we were kept in custody under the law, being shut up to the faith which was later to be revealed. Therefore the law has become our tutor to lead us to Christ, so that we may be justified by faith. But now that faith has come, we are no longer under a tutor (NASB).

> Before this faith came, we were held prisoners by the law, locked up until faith should be revealed. So the law was put in charge to lead us to Christ [put in charge until Christ came – footnote] that we might be justified by faith. Now that faith has come, we are no longer under the supervision of the law (NIV).

> Before faith came, we were held captive under the law, imprisoned until the coming faith would be revealed. So then, the law was our guardian until Christ came, in order that we might be justified by faith. But now that faith has come, we are no longer under a guardian (ESV).

All these versions have in-built problems of one sort or another, problems which have led many to seriously misunderstand the apostle. And the consequences have been severe. I want to do what I can about it.[1]

First, 'faith' (Gal. 3:23,25). Paul was not speaking about 'faith' as a personal experience – that is, 'believing'. Rather, he was speaking of 'the faith' as the gospel, Christ – that is, 'who and what is to be believed'. In other words, 'faith' here is objective, not subjective.

Secondly, 'to bring us' (Gal. 3:24, NKJV, AV), 'to lead us' (NASB, NIV). These words are not in the original, and should be removed. They have been the unfortunate source of much misunderstanding. Paul did not say the law was given as a child-custodian 'to bring us' or 'to lead us' to Christ. Rather, the law was in place as a child-custodian 'until' the coming of Christ (Gal. 3:19). The ESV got it right: 'the law was... until Christ came'.

Thirdly, the 'tutor' (Gal. 3:24), Greek *paidagōgos,* 'tutor' (NKJV), 'schoolmaster' (AV), 'in charge' (NIV), 'tutor', literally 'child-conductor' (NASB), 'guardian' (ESV). Sadly, some of these translations (especially, 'schoolmaster' and 'tutor'), even the transliteration 'pedagogue', give the misleading impression that the law was an 'educator', much like *didaskalos* (Rom. 2:20; Heb. 5:2, for example). *This* is not the meaning of *paidagōgos.* The word is a combination of *pais* (child) and *agōgos* (leader), derived from *agō,* 'to drive, to lead by laying hold of, to conduct' with the idea of discipline. As Thayer explained: 'The name was applied to trustworthy slaves who were charged with the duty of supervising the life and morals of boys... The boys were not allowed so much as to step out of the house without them, before reaching the age of manhood... The name carries with it an idea of severity (as of a stern censor and enforcer of morals)'. And, linking this with the previous point, the child-custodian's job was not to *bring* the immature boy anywhere; rather, he had to discipline and protect the boy *until* he reached maturity. During that time, the Jews

---

[1] For more, see my *Christ,* especially pp127-140,348-358,420-430.

were 'kept under the law, shut up' (Gal. 3:23, AV), 'were held prisoners by the law, locked up' by the law (NIV), 'held captive under the law, imprisoned' (ESV), 'kept under guard by the law' (NKJV), confined by the law.[2]

Fourthly, what 'law' was Paul speaking of? There is no room for doubt. None whatever. Paul was speaking of the entire Mosaic institution. He was not speaking of the moral law, the ceremonial law or the judicial law, allowing the terms for the moment.[3] Nor was he speaking of Jewish misunderstanding of the law, or legalism. Paul said 'the law' and he meant the law, the law of Moses in its entirety. *And he kept to it throughout the passage.*[4]

Fifthly, what of the 'added'? This word must not be misunderstood. The law 'was added' to God's promise to Abraham, given 430 years before the law (Gal. 3:19). Paul did not say that the law was 'incorporated' into the promise, or added to the promise in the sense that the pair made one covenant, a covenant of grace. Quite the opposite, in fact. The law came in as something extra to the promise, a distinct, separate and subordinate economy or system, *not* an alteration of, an adjustment to, or modifier of the promise. The law did not belong to the existing system or promise. It was not part of it. It was something additional, not fundamental. It was an add-on.[5] As the apostle said: 'The law entered' (Rom. 5:20). The Greek word for 'entered' is used only twice in the New Testament (Rom. 5:20; Gal. 2:4). In the latter, it means

---

[2] I was a modern pedagogue – a Mathematics teacher – for years, but if I had acted the part of a real pedagogue, the State would have taken me to court for child abuse!

[3] Not that I do allow them! Scripture doesn't! See my *Christ* pp100-104,392-400.

[4] Some Reformed commentators are ambiguous on this, or change their mind as they go along, without justification – except to maintain their covenant theology at all costs (including distortion of the text by not allowing Paul to speak for himself).

[5] It was also temporary (see below), something very different to the promise, which was permanent.

'sneaked in'. While in Romans 5:20 it does not bear the evil sense of Galatians 2:4, nevertheless it possesses the connotation, 'slipped in between', 'came in besides', 'in addition to'. The law slipped in. Paul's emphasis on the law's temporary place in salvation history is obvious here.[6] It ought to be unmistakable.

The apostle went further. Do not forget the Judaisers' claim that the Abrahamic and Mosaic covenants were one and the same.[7] Paul did not fudge the issue. They could not be more wrong. He was adamant. Going for the jugular, he categorically *contrasted* the two covenants, and let all concerned – the Galatians and the Judaisers – know the consequence of denying the contrast: 'For if the inheritance is of the law, it is no longer of promise' (Gal. 3:18). This he confirmed in Galatians 4:24-26, where he argued that the Abrahamic covenant and the Mosaic covenant were two separate, distinct, covenants, not two parts of the same. What is more, throughout the letter to the Galatians, Paul stoutly preserved this separateness, standing firm against the Judaisers who, as I say, wanted to blend the promise and the law into one.[8]

There is no question but that Paul was thinking of the law's vital, though temporary, role in the unfolding of salvation history. That history is not flat, nor smoothly evolutionary in character. Rather, it is the record of God's interventions. God broke into the history of the world to give Abraham the promise. 430 years later, he intervened again to give Israel the law through Moses. Centuries later, at the right time (Gal. 4:4), he intervened again and sent his Son, the Seed (Gal. 3:19). He

---

[6] See my comments on salvation history in my *Christ* pp30-35.

[7] For more on the Judaisers, see my *Christ* pp16-18. The modern equivalent are the Reformed who, holding to Calvin's three uses of the law, claim that unbelievers must have the law preached to them to prepare them for Christ (preparationism), and believers must be under the law for sanctification.

[8] This, of course, puts the Reformed advocates firmly on the side of those Paul was speaking against!

intervened again with the gift of the Spirit (Acts 2).[9] To lose sight of Paul's eschatological argument is tragic.[10]

Moreover, as with the previous point, Paul was speaking about the law – the law in its entirety, the law full stop! It was the law, the whole law, that was added 430 years after the promise, and it was the law, the whole law that was temporary in that God intended it to last until the coming of the Seed. There is not the slightest hint that Paul was saying the whole law was given at Sinai, two thirds of which lasted until the coming of the Seed, the remaining one third being eternal.[11]

Sixthly, the 'us'. When Paul said: 'Christ has redeemed *us* from the curse of the law, having become a curse for *us*' (Gal. 3:13), to whom was he referring? Was he speaking of elect Jews? Or was he speaking of the elect, full stop, both Jews and Gentiles? There are strong arguments for both. The problem of the 'us' is not confined to Galatians 3:13-14, of course. It also arises in Galatians 3:23-29 and 4:3-7. It is likely that Paul was speaking primarily of elect Jews – and this is where the emphasis must fall – yet encompassing all the elect, both Jew and Gentile, in Christ's redemption.[12] While historically and actually it was only the Jews who could be said to be 'under the law', Paul

---

[9] There is one more intervention to come; Christ's return.

[10] See Isa. 34:4; 65:17; Hag. 2:6-9,21-23; Heb. 12:25-29; 2 Pet 3:3-7. This, of course, takes us to the continuity/discontinuity debate. See my *Christ* pp76-79,374-380.

[11] Actually, less than 1% of it.

[12] The arguments in favour of viewing the 'us' as Jews can be summarised thus: while all men, both Jew and Gentile, are sinners, since it was only the Jews who were under the law, its curse could only apply to them, and therefore redemption from the law could apply only to them; since Gentiles are spoken of in Gal. 3:14, it is likely that the Jews were being spoken of in Gal. 3:13; Paul said 'we who are Jews' (Gal. 2:15); note the us/you contrast of Gal. 3:23-25 and 3:26-29; and, finally, the contrast in the Greek between 'us' and 'the Gentiles'.

probably included the Gentiles on the basis of Romans 2:14-15.[13]

And, *seventhly*, do not miss the unity which the apostle stresses in this passage. The Seed is one (Gal. 3:16), God is one (Gal. 3:20), and believers (whether Jew or Greek) 'are all one in Christ Jesus' (Gal. 3:28). In short, Gentiles do not need to go under the law to belong to the people of God, or to ratify their belonging to that people. They should pay no attention to the Judaisers who want them to submit to the law to make them 'kosher'. In Christ, they, along with believing Jews, 'are all sons of God through faith in Christ Jesus'. They, *all* of them, have 'put on Christ', 'are Christ's', and 'are Abraham's seed, and heirs according to the promise' (Gal. 3:26-29), and that without the law.[14]

---

[13] See my *Christ* pp27-37,337-347 for my reasons. Perhaps Paul was treating the Jews as a special case of redemption (Matt. 15:24; John 4:22), or in their priority over the Gentiles in its order (Luke 24:47; John 1:11; Acts 1:8; 3:26; 10:36; 13:26,46; 28:28; Rom. 1:16; 2:9). As I showed in my *Christ* pp47-48,342-347, it may be that Israel and the law served as a paradigm for Gentiles; the Gentiles are answerable to God for the moral standards he has placed upon them and within them, just as Israel was answerable for the law. This is why the Old Testament prophets could condemn the nations for their failure, just as they could condemn Israel for hers – even though the Gentiles and Israel were not under the same law. And this might be the explanation of Paul's warning in Gal. 4:21 and 5:4. For unbelievers, God's 'law' – whatever form it may take – continues to condemn those who are not in Christ and thus have not fulfilled the law. And whatever the arguments over the *us* in Gal. 3, in any event all men need redemption since 'they are all under sin', 'the Scripture has confined all under sin' (Rom. 3:9,22-23; 11:32; Gal. 3:22). All men – Jews and Gentiles – are slaves to sin. See my comments on Rom. 3:19 in my *Christ* pp35-37,339-341.

[14] Gal. 3:20 has baffled most, if not all, commentators. While I have strong objections to N.T.Wright's theology on several vital issues (see my *Conversion*; *Hinge*), I like the following: 'Moses, to whom the Galatians are being tempted to look for membership in the true people of God, is not the one through whom that single family is brought about... The law cannot be God's final word: God, being himself one, desires a single family, but the Mosaic law was given to one race only

hand there is an annulling of the former commandment because of its weakness and unprofitableness... On the other hand, there is the bringing in of a better hope... For if that first covenant had been faultless, then no place would have been sought for a second... In that [God] says: "A new covenant", he has made the first obsolete' (Heb. 7:18-19; 8:7,13). 'The letter kills, but the Spirit gives life. But if the ministry of death, written and engraved on stones, was glorious... how will the ministry of the Spirit not be more glorious? For if the ministry of condemnation had glory, the ministry of righteousness exceeds much more in glory' (2 Cor. 3:6-9).

All this is reinforced by Paul's use of 'pedagogue'. The pedagogue was a guardian, a child-custodian, whose job it was to restrain a minor from immoral behaviour, and to protect him until he matured. Once the juvenile reached maturity, however, the pedagogue's work was finished. He had no more say over his former trainee. He was out of a job, surplus to requirements. His old power and rule had ended. Paul used this well-known practice to illustrate the law's relationship to the Jews, standing over them, keeping them in line throughout the age of the law.[19] The Mosaic order (the old-covenant administration, economy, dispensation), the law, was the pedagogue which kept Israel in order until the coming of Christ and his new covenant.[20] Once Christ had come, however, believing Jews were no longer under the law (Gal. 3:25). And if Jewish believers are no longer under the law, then, of course, neither are Gentile believers.

Note the repetition of 'under' – the key word – in '*under* guard by the law', '*under* a [child-custodian]', '*under* guardians

---

[19] As I have noted, all this is reinforced by Paul's use of the guardian or steward in Gal. 4:1-7.

[20] See Acts 15. Note the *our fathers nor we* (Acts 15:10) – clearly a reference to the Jews; Peter, a Jew, was speaking about the Jews. Note the reference in Acts 15:21 to synagogues and sabbaths; clearly Jewish – not Gentile – terms. The law distinguished between – divided indeed (Eph. 2:14-15) (see my *Christ* pp27-37,200-207,337-341,478-480 – Jews and Gentiles, but grace, through trust in Christ, makes them one (Acts 15:7-9; see also John 10:16; 11:52; 17:20-24; Gal. 3:28; Eph. 2:13-22).

and stewards' and '*under* the elements of the world', and '*under* the law' (Gal. 3:23,25; 4:2-3,5). The repetition of 'under', and the thrust of the argument, show these phrases are all saying one and the same thing. Which is? The law, bringing in and imposing rules, governed and guarded the way the Jews behaved, confining them *under* itself. The law was over the Jews, they were *under* it, *under* its grip, *under* its power. It revealed sin, and aroused or stimulated it. Paul says the same thing in Romans 6 and 7. In both Galatians and Romans, the apostle makes it as clear as noonday that there are two stages of salvation history. The former age, 'under law', and the present age, under Christ, 'under grace'. The apostle always heavily contrasts the two. The former age was the age or realm of bondage; the latter, freedom. Now when Paul spoke of 'being under the law', he meant more than being under its curse.[21] He meant being under *it*, under the law as a system, under it as a realm, under it as a rule of behaviour, under the law as a child-custodian, under its reign, under its grip, under its power. It is all a question of maturity, of age, epoch, realm and status. To be under the law is to be under a child-custodian, whereas to be under Christ is to be free. Just as a mature man is no longer under the child-custodian, so the believer is no longer under the law, no longer subject to the imposition of its rule.[22]

And since this is so, how can believers think of going under the law? After all, the child-custodian only had a job while the child was immature. When the child reached maturity, not only the child-custodian's work, but the child-custodian himself, was finished. Well then, as Paul states so clearly, believers are 'all sons of God through faith in Christ Jesus' (Gal. 3:26). Sons? The apostle uses *huioi* – grown up, mature, sons. And he

---

[21] This, of course, is a common ploy adopted by the Reformed, which, coupled with their almost incessant use of the non-scriptural 'the ceremonial law', marks their determined (but desperate) attempt to evade the plain meaning of the apostle's words.

[22] This does not mean that the believer has nothing at all to do with the law, but the law is not the rule nor norm for defining his walk with God. See my *Christ* pp289-294,530-540 to see how the law plays the role of a believer's paradigm as part of 2 Tim. 3:16-17.

attempt to be justified by law; you have fallen from grace' (Gal. 5:4). 'If by grace, then it is no longer of works; otherwise grace is no longer grace' (Rom. 11:6).[30] How, as many claim, the Mosaic covenant can be thought to be one and the same as the Abrahamic covenant, or that it is 'a fresh administration of the covenant of grace', defies common sense. Worse, it defies Scripture: 'The letter kills, but the Spirit gives life. But if the ministry of death, written and engraved on stones, was glorious... how will the ministry of the Spirit not be more glorious? For if the ministry of condemnation had glory, the ministry of righteousness exceeds much more in glory' (2 Cor. 3:6-9).

As I have already observed, very often we can test our understanding of Paul by looking at the questions he raises after making his staggering assertions. Paul frequently raised objections to his doctrine – we shall meet it again – and here is a case in point. I draw your attention, reader, in particular, to Paul's use of the word 'then': 'What purpose *then* does the law serve?... Is the law *then* against the promises of God?' (Gal. 3:19,21). In other words, Paul said, in light of my [Paul's] teaching – which, I admit, sounds so startling – how *then* does the law square with the promise? Now, if the commonly-held Reformed view is right, and the law and the gospel comprise one covenant, if it is essential to preach the law to sinners before preaching the gospel, and if it is essential to take sinners, once converted, back to the law to sanctify them, Paul would never have asked such a (redundant) question as: 'What purpose then does the law serve?' 'Why the law then?' (NASB). Such a question could be raised only by someone who knows the two systems are very different, whose teaching has exposed the difference, and yet who needs to make sure his readers do not denigrate the law. No one who teaches the standard Reformed view needs to ask such a question. It simply does not arise. Nor would his hearers ever think of it. It would

---

[30] Pointing out the obvious – that in Gal. 5:4 Paul was speaking about justification – cuts no ice. The point I am making at this stage is irrefutable – law and grace are contrasted.

never cross their mind. Under his teaching, they are never exposed to thinking the law is different to grace, since he has taught them that the law and the gospel are virtually one and the same covenant. If a Reformed teacher did ask such a question, he would surely be shouted down, dismissed: 'As we all know – and, after all, as *you* taught us – the law serves to prepare the sinner for Christ, and to sanctify the saint. That's the law's purpose. You yourself told us! So why are you asking such a daft question?' Consequently, the fact that Paul raised this very question, using the word 'then', and yet did not give the 'standard' answer, proves he was no advocate of the Reformed first and third uses of the law. Far from it! The truth is, he had to explain how the law fitted in with the promise. The law, he said, was temporary, confining the Jews until Christ came. Thus it is the historical setting of Galatians 3:10-25 which must be grasped. It must not be lost in a welter of words about preaching the law to pagan sinners today. *Do not miss the big picture.*

In the apostle's question, the word 'serve' is not in the original. The original reads: 'Why then the law?' The 'serve' has been added by translators. Very well. But what tense should they have chosen? Is it: 'What purpose *did* the law serve?' Or: 'What purpose *does* the law *now* serve?' The context speaks of the past. This seems, to put it no stronger, to teach that the law has no ongoing function for the believer. But if Paul did ask: 'What purpose *does* the law *now* serve?', why ever did he not reply along the lines of Calvin's threefold use of the law? Why did the Spirit leave it for 1500 years until he made it known to the churches through the Reformer? This is not the same as saying men cannot discuss a problem before it arises – for instance, John Owen did not tackle 'being slain in the Spirit' – for Paul was dealing with the precise issue in hand at this very point. And he was inspired. So why did he not give the classic Reformed answer?

We may put it to the test. Ask any Reformed teacher to tell us the purpose of the law, and he will rattle off Calvin's threefold use. Now ask Paul! Well...?

We may go further. As I have emphasised, the era of the law was temporary.[31] It was only an interlude (but a God-ordained interlude, I hasten to add) in God's great plan for the ages. And God gave Moses the law with the intention that it should last only until the establishment of the new covenant by Christ (Gal. 3:16-19,24-25).[32] The entire law, not the law's 'mode of administration', was abolished by the coming of Christ.

As for the law of Moses being temporary, note the following: 'In that [God] says: "A new covenant", he has made the first obsolete. Now what is becoming obsolete and growing old is ready to vanish away' (Heb. 8:13; see also 2 Cor. 3:11,13). As for 'vanish away', the same root-word is used in: 'What is your life? It is even a vapour that appears for a little time and then vanishes away' (Jas. 4:14). This opens up an interesting parallel between the temporary nature of the law and the limited, temporary life-span of man: 'The days of our lives are seventy years' (Ps. 90:10). As soon as we are born, we begin to die. 'As for man, his days are like grass; as a flower of the field, so he flourishes. For the wind passes over it, and it is gone, and its place remembers it no more' (Ps. 103:15-16). 'Man is like a breath; his days are like a passing shadow' (Ps. 144:4; see Job 8:9-10; 14:1-2,5-6; Ps. 39:5-6,11-12; 78:39; 89:47; 90:5-6; 1 Pet. 1:24; *etc.*). Our days are 'numbered' (Job 14:5; Ps. 90:12). Similarly, the law of Moses came with a 'sell-by' date stamped on it; it was a temporary, passing shadow which, when its God-appointed task was done, at God's predestined time it would vanish away. And with the coming of Christ and his accomplishment of his Father's purpose, the law's work was over, completed and fulfilled. The age of the law had passed. In addition to this temporary aspect, there is

---

[31] The law of God is eternal; the law of Moses was temporary. See my *Christ* pp222,227.

[32] I am not suggesting for a moment that God changed his mind, that his intention in giving the law was thwarted, or anything remotely like it. God always did intend to bring in the law, *but only as a temporary measure.*

also a parallel – a connection, indeed – between the *frailty* of man and the *weakness* of the law (Rom. 8:3).[33]

I have spent some time on this section of Galatians because its importance can scarcely be exaggerated. As I have said repeatedly, *do not miss the big picture.* I have laboured the point simply because many Reformed writers claim the two covenants (law and grace) are one and the same, and because they build so much upon it.[34] The fact is, the view we take of Galatians 3:19-20 will largely determine how we think of the believer and the law. Recall Paul's argument thus far. In dealing with the Judaisers, their claim that the covenants are one and the same, and their call for the believers to go under the law, he has drawn on the Galatians' experience. He has appealed to Scripture. He has called upon human reason in using an analogy from everyday life (Gal. 3:15) and applied it to God's dealings with men. He has explicitly set out the temporary nature of the law's reign. He has proved that the Galatians already have all they need spiritually – God's promise, the Christ, and the Spirit – and they have it without the law. How can they think of going to the law in face of the evidence he has produced? What purpose could it serve? The law's sun has set. But, it must be noticed, in light of this, Paul has to answer the question, if this really is the state of things, why then was the law given in the first place? And this is the very question Paul raises and answers. In truth, he has already answered it. The law was not given to believers in the age of the gospel. It was given to Jews before the coming of Christ. And those Jews had to live under the bondage of that law, even though it did not give them any power to meet its demands. But now that Christ has come, that age is over. The law has ceased. It has not ceased in part or to certain ends. It has ceased. The law, the age of the law, is over. With the coming of Christ, salvation history has entered a new age, the age of the Spirit. Israel's pedagogue, the law, has gone; the Spirit has come. And it is the Holy Spirit, not the law as a pedagogue, who sanctifies

---

[33] See my *Christ* pp172-176,460-464 on the 'weakness' of the law.
[34] See my *Christ* pp75-98,369-391.

the believer. The verb 'led' in Galatians 5:18 comes from the same word as 'pedagogue' – an example of Paul's love of wordplay.[35] The believer is 'pedagogued' by the Spirit, not the law, now that in the fullness of time Christ has come, and the Spirit has been given. The law's time is finished. Now is the age of the Spirit; now is the time for walking in and by the Spirit.[36]

To sum up Galatians 3:10-25: the law was given through Moses, it was given to Israel, it was given because of sin, it imprisoned and disciplined those under it, it was never intended to be permanent, but to last only until the coming of Christ. And this is why I offer my rendering of Galatians 3:23-24:

> Before the new covenant came, we were held captive under the law, imprisoned until the coming new covenant would be revealed. So then, the law was our child custodian until Christ came, in order that we might be justified by faith. But now that the new covenant has come, we are no longer under a child custodian.

How can it be thought that a believer ought to go under the law? To make Gentile believers in the new covenant conform to the law of the old covenant, which was intended to discipline unregenerate Jews in the age before the coming of Christ, is nothing short of incredible.

May I say it just once more. I address all believers. We are given the big picture in Galatians 3. *Do not miss it!* The doctrine the apostle sets out here is of massive importance. Having seen it, do not forget it. Do not allow any man, however illustrious he may be (Ps. 118:9; 146:3,5), to impose any template on Scripture. In particular, do not let yourself be robbed of the apostle's teaching by submitting to the covenant-theology construct which was forged in the 16th century. If you do – or if you have – you will find yourself imprisoned under

---

[35] In addition to Gal. 3:24 with 5:18, see Rom. 8:2-4; 9:6; 1 Cor. 9:19-23; 11:3-16; Gal. 6:2,16, and so on.

[36] This is not to say the law has no place at all in the life of the believer. See my *Christ* pp279-298,528-542.

the law for both assurance and sanctification. As a result, you will be cheated of your rightful birthright as a believer – the liberty, the glory and the joy that are in Christ.

There is one lesson above all that we should take from Galatians 3:10-25, as for every passage of Scripture (Luke 24:37,32,45): Look for Christ. Look *to* Christ. For Christ is all (Col. 3:11).

Before Christ came, the Jews were imprisoned under the law, kept there until he came. But Christ has come, and he has established the new covenant. Those who trust Christ are justified by faith. Not only that, in establishing the new covenant, Christ fulfilled and abolished the old, so that believers, having died to the law, are no longer under that killing ministry, but are alive in the Spirit:

> Therefore, my brethren, you also have become dead to the law through the body of Christ, that you may be married to another – to him who was raised from the dead, that we should bear fruit to God. For when we were in the flesh, the sinful passions which were aroused by the law were at work in our members to bear fruit to death. But now we have been delivered from the law, having died to what we were held by, so that we should serve in the newness of the Spirit and not in the oldness of the letter... For the law of the Spirit of life in Christ Jesus has made me free from the law of sin and death. For what the law could not do in that it was weak through the flesh, God did by sending his own Son in the likeness of sinful flesh, on account of sin: he condemned sin in the flesh, that the righteous requirement of the law might be fulfilled in us who do not walk according to the flesh but according to the Spirit (Rom. 7:4-6; 8:2-4).

> I through the law died to the law that I might live to God. I have been crucified with Christ; it is no longer I who live, but Christ lives in me; and the life which I now live in the flesh I live by faith in the Son of God, who loved me and gave himself for me (Gal. 2:19-20).

Believer, this is your birthright. Realise it. Count on it (Rom. 6:11). Enjoy it.

Appendix 3
The Invisible 'But' of John 1:17

The law was given through Moses, but grace and truth came through Jesus Christ.

God gave Israel the law through Moses (John 7:19); and we know why: 'The law entered that the offence might abound' (Rom. 5:20). He also gave Israel the law to predict and foreshadow the coming of Christ and the new covenant (Deut. 18:15-18; Col. 2:16-17; Heb. 3:5; 8:5; 10:1). Then, in the fullness of time, God sent his Son into the world, born under the law (Mark 1:15; Gal. 4:4), in order to redeem those under the law; that is, to redeem the elect, adopt them as his sons and give them his Spirit as a witness (Gal. 4:5-6). In short: God sent grace into the world by his Son, Jesus Christ (John 1:14; Tit. 2:11-14). And we know why: 'But where sin abounded, grace abounded much more, so that as sin reigned in death, even so grace might reign through righteousness to eternal life through Jesus Christ our Lord' (Rom. 5:20-21).[1]

Paul did not leave it there. He went on to set out the glories of that reigning grace in Christ:

> Therefore, my brethren, you also have become dead to the law through the body of Christ, that you may be married to another – to him who was raised from the dead, that we should bear fruit to God. For when we were in the flesh, the sinful passions which were aroused by the law were at work in our members to bear fruit to death. But now we have been delivered from the law, having died to what we were held by, so that we should serve in the newness of the Spirit and not in the oldness of the letter... There is therefore now no condemnation to those who are in Christ Jesus, who do not walk according to the flesh, but according to the Spirit. For the law of the Spirit of life in Christ Jesus has made me free from the law of sin and death. For what the law could not do in that it was weak

---

[1] When I first published this as an article the title was 'The "But"' of John 1:17: Absent but Vital'.

149

through the flesh, God did by sending his own Son in the likeness of sinful flesh, on account of sin: he condemned sin in the flesh, that the righteous requirement of the law might be fulfilled in us who do not walk according to the flesh but according to the Spirit... As many as are led by the Spirit of God, these are sons of God. For you did not receive the spirit of bondage again to fear, but you received the Spirit of adoption by whom we cry out: 'Abba, Father'. The Spirit himself bears witness with our spirit that we are children of God, and if children, then heirs – heirs of God and joint heirs with Christ (Rom. 7:4-6; 8:1-4,14-17).

What a contrast, law and grace! What a contrast, Moses and Christ (Heb. 3:1-6)! And how wonderfully John shines the spotlight on the contrast: 'The law was given through Moses, but grace and truth came through Jesus Christ' (John 1:17)! The translators did not use the word *but* for nothing in John 1:17. The apostle points to a very definite, clear, unmistakable contrast between law and grace.

   He is not alone:

There is an annulling of the former commandment because of its weakness and unprofitableness... There is the bringing in of a better hope... For if that first covenant had been faultless, then no place would have been sought for a second... In that [God] says: 'A new covenant', he has made the first obsolete (Heb. 7:18-19; 8:7,13).

In short:

The letter kills, but the Spirit gives life. But if the ministry of death, written and engraved on stones, was glorious... how will the ministry of the Spirit not be more glorious? For if the ministry of condemnation had glory, the ministry of righteousness exceeds much more in glory (2 Cor. 3:6-9).[2]

Yet, despite all this weight of evidence, Reformed writers seldom give John 1:17 proper consideration in their works on the law. How sad this is! Worse, some have gone so far as to deny the apostle's contrast between law! There is no contradiction between law and grace, so it is said. Even the *but*

---

[2] For more on all this, see my *Christ* pp113-115,409-411.

in John 1:17 has been dismissed as a delusion – a 'will o'the wisp'.[3]

How sad is this. How wrong!

True, there is no 'but' in the Greek,[4] but this is far from conclusive. It is certainly there in spirit and by implication. In fact, the lack of the stated 'but' makes its presence even more felt. Its absence speaks louder than its (obvious) inclusion; the finesse in John's turn of phrase would have been blunted by the inclusion of the 'but'. Therefore, although precisely catching the spirit of John's words, our translators, in trying to help us more readily understand the apostle, by introducing the 'but', they have, in fact, taken some of the subtlety out of what he wrote. But whether in print, or in our head, the 'but' has to be understood.

Let me prove it. Take: 'God be thanked that *though* you were the slaves of sin, yet you obeyed from the heart that form of doctrine to which you were delivered' (Rom. 6:17). To omit the *though* would be tantamount to making Paul say he was glad his readers had been the slaves of sin, when, in fact, he was thankful that *even though* they had been the slaves of sin, they had nevertheless obeyed the gospel. His argument hinges entirely on the *though*. If anybody dismisses the *though* as an English will o' the wisp, a mere technicality of the language, he virtually destroys what Paul actually said. Yet there is no 'though' in the Greek text! As with the 'but' in John 1:17, its absence speaks volumes.

Similarly: 'Though he was a Son, *yet* he learned obedience by the things which he suffered' (Heb. 5:8). The *yet* is supplied, it is not in the original Greek, but by no stretch of the imagination can it be dismissed as trivial. In fact, its inclusion emphasises the amazing nature of what is being said. It is the most important word in the verse, even though the writer did not use it. Though Jesus was the Son of God, *even so,*

---

[3] Are 2 Cor. 3:11; Heb. 7:18; 8:13 more of these 'will o'the wisps'?
[4] The NIV, strictly correct here, left it out.

staggeringly, even he, yet he – he of all people – learned obedience by the things which he suffered.

A few more examples must suffice: 'Beloved, do not avenge yourselves, but *rather* give place to wrath' (Rom. 12:19). The *rather* gives the proper emphasis, but it is not in the original. Again, try leaving out the second *must* in John 3:30, *his* in John 6:52 (*his* is vital – any butcher can provide meat, but how could Jesus provide *his* own flesh for them to eat?), *as for* in John 9:29, *that is* in Ephesians 2:15, *rather* in 1 Timothy 4:7 (AV), *and escape* in 2 Timothy 2:26 (the verse becomes nonsense otherwise), *because* in 2 Timothy 4:3; and so on. None of these words are in the Greek!

Returning to John 1:17 – as I said, the *but* being left out, the verse is even more starkly powerful and blunt: 'The law was given through Moses; grace and truth came through Jesus Christ'. In fact, we could – maybe, we should – use a full stop: 'The law was given through Moses. Grace and truth came through Jesus Christ'.

Clearly, however, a word or phrase is implied in the text, and has to be supplied. Reader, you may use *but*, or *whereas*, or *on the other hand,* or *in contrast.* You choose!

In addition, the context of John 1:17 demands the contrast. Read John 1:8,11-13,20. Above all, read John 1:18. There is no *but*, literally, in between the two sentences: 'No one has seen God at any time. The only begotten Son, who is in the bosom of the Father, he has declared him'. Notwithstanding the lack of 'but', who would not agree that John here draws a remarkable contrast? In the past age – the age of law – God did not show his glory as now he has in the age of the gospel. Do not miss the eschatological 'but now' of Romans 3:21 once again.[5]

Let me take another passage of Scripture to underline the point. I refer to Hebrews 9. The inspired writer, opening the chapter with an exposition of the first or old covenant, soon sounds the note of its uselessness to cleanse the conscience (Heb. 9:1-10). 'It was symbolic... imposed until the time of reformation' (Heb. 9:9-10), 'an illustration... applying until the

---

[5] See my *Christ* pp76-79,378-379.

time of the new order' (NIV). What was this new order, this 'reformation'? It was the coming of Christ, the gospel. How does the writer to the Hebrews state this fact? 'But Christ came', he said (Heb. 9:11), 'when Christ came' (NIV). These words should not be mumbled. They should be thundered: **'But Christ came'!** 'When Christ came'! And the NIV caught the dramatic, stupendous sense of change at this watershed of the ages, exquisitely grasping the point of the 'now' in Hebrews 9:15: 'Christ is the mediator of a new covenant, that those who are called may receive the promised eternal inheritance – *now* that he has died as a ransom to set them free from the sins committed under the first covenant'. Once again, it is the eschatological 'but now', the great turning point of the ages. The shadow has gone, the reality has come. The external is finished, the inward is established. The weak is displaced by the mighty. The useless has been abolished by the effectual. It is John 1:17.

It is wrong to say that the gospel is a *clearer* way of salvation than the law. It is a *different* way, chalk and cheese! It will not do to say that John 1:17 *seems* to speak of the inferiority of the law when compared to the gospel. It does no such thing. The verse teaches that law and grace are very different things, two ages which are strongly contrasted. There is a distinction – more, an antithesis, an opposition, a contradiction – between the two, even as some Reformed writers admit, on occasion at great length.

Many Reformed commentators, however, are weak on the verse, or use their escape routes to say John was speaking about justification only, or about the ceremonial law. Furthermore, they are not averse to trying to uphold their system – that is, an excessive emphasis upon the continuity of the Testaments – by qualifying John, adding the proviso that, while, of course, the law *was* given through Moses, and grace and truth on the other hand *did come* by Jesus Christ, nevertheless, Moses brought some grace, and, in any case, believers are still under the moral law as a perfect rule of life.

John, of course, said nothing of the sort. What he said was: 'The law was given through Moses, but grace and truth came through Jesus Christ'. And the verse says what it means, and means what it says to the reader of plain English. And it is full of contrast.

As I have said, by leaving out the 'but' John makes his point even stronger: 'The law was given through Moses. Grace and truth came through Jesus Christ'. Leaving out the 'but' actually lays more stress on the *grace*, and emphasises the contrast between that and *law*. It lays more stress on the *came*, and emphasises the contrast between that and the *given*. It lays more stress on *Jesus Christ*, and emphasises the contrast between him and *Moses*:

The **law** was **given** through **Moses**
Grace and truth **came** through **Jesus Christ**

What is more, from John 1:17 we learn that whereas the law *was given through* Moses, Christ *brought* grace. Note the passive/active contrast. Note the contrast between *given* and *brought*. Above all, it is not simply that Moses *received* one thing, and Christ *brought* something else. Both Moses and Christ are associated with covenants, but the difference between their covenants is vast. Moses was given *the law*; Christ brought *grace*. Moses was given *God's* law; Christ brought *his own* grace. Moses was given the old covenant; Christ brought the new. Moses' covenant was written on stone; Christ's is written in the heart. It is not just that Christ gives his people the gospel, and Moses gave the Jews the law. Christ gives his people *grace*, he gives his people a *heart* to love his gospel, but Moses could offer no power to keep the law. This contrast of covenants is a major aspect of the debate on the believer, the law and sanctification.

Small as John 1:17 may appear to be, it plays a vital role in the question of the believer and the law. Any work which fails to take proper account of what it teaches, can hardly be considered a serious attempt to get to grips with the biblical evidence on the subject.

Appendix 4
Hebrews

If any book in the New Testament disproves the Reformed idea that the Sinai covenant and the new covenant are one and the same, it must be Hebrews, which makes it clear beyond a doubt that these two covenants are very different – indeed, that they are mutually exclusive – and that the Mosaic covenant has been abolished in Christ.[1] I will be brief on this – having dealt with it elsewhere[2] – but since it has large implications for the issue of the believer and the law, and since Hebrews deals with it so fully, it would be wrong not to take at least a glance at what it says on the two covenants.

But before I get to individual passages, may I suggest, reader, that you read (aloud) Hebrews 7:11 – 10:18? May I further suggest that you read it again, in a version or two different to the one you normally use? To my mind, the argument is overwhelming. We have a new covenant, a new priesthood, a new order, a new system, a new sacrifice, a new commandment... new everything. Except, according to Reformed teaching, the law! And yet the law is the covenant, and the covenant is the law! Whatever else is new under the new covenant, it must be the law! Hebrews 7:11 – 10:18, I say, is irrefutable evidence that it is so.

Now for individual passages.

Take Hebrews 2:1-4, which reads:

> Therefore we must give the more earnest heed to the things we have heard, lest we drift away. For if the word spoken through angels proved steadfast, and every transgression and disobedience received a just reward, how shall we escape if we neglect so great a salvation, which at the first began to be spoken by the Lord, and was confirmed to us by those who heard him, God also bearing witness both with signs and

---

[1] For extracts, see my *Christ* pp476-477.
[2] See my *Battle*; *Infant*; *The Priesthood*.

wonders, with various miracles, and gifts of the Holy Spirit, according to his own will?

Note the contrast drawn between what 'we have heard' and 'the word spoken through angels'. The writer, clearly, was referring to the gospel and the law. As a consequence, let me start again. Note the contrast drawn between the two covenants, and note, further, just how stark this contrast is. And we are talking of the contrast between the gospel and the law, between the new and the old covenants. One covenant is 'the things [which] we have heard... so great a salvation', which is the gospel. The other is 'the word spoken through angels', which is the law (Acts 7:53; Gal. 3:19). The old covenant was concerned with 'transgression and disobedience' in that every sin 'received a just reward' or retribution or penalty. The new covenant is also concerned with sin, but instead of bringing punishment, it brings salvation. The contrast could not be more sharply made. The new covenant is far superior to the old, and that is why 'we must give the *more* earnest heed to the things *we* have heard', since these things are so much better than what was heard under the Mosaic covenant. If this point is ignored, many errors ensue. Confusion over the believer and the law is one such.

Take Hebrews 7:11-22 and 8:6-13:

> Of necessity there is also a change of the law... On the one hand there is an annulling of the former commandment because of its weakness and unprofitableness, for the law made nothing perfect; on the other hand, there is the bringing in of a better hope, through which we draw near to God... Jesus has become a surety of a better covenant... But now[3] he has obtained a more excellent ministry, inasmuch as he is also mediator of a better covenant, which was established on better promises. For if that first covenant had been faultless, then no place would have been sought for a second. Because finding fault with them, he says: 'Behold, the days are coming, says the LORD, when I will make a new covenant with the house of Israel and with the house of Judah – not according to the covenant that I made with their fathers in the day when I took

---

[3] Note the 'but now'.

them by the hand to lead them out of the land of Egypt... This is the covenant that I will make... I will put my laws in their mind and write them on their hearts...'. In that [God] says: 'A new covenant', he has made the first obsolete. Now what is becoming obsolete and growing old is ready to vanish away.

If these words are not plain enough, I fear nothing will suffice. Once again, a clear contrast is drawn between the two covenants. On the one hand, we have 'the first covenant', 'the law', 'the former commandment'. And on the other 'a second', 'a better covenant which was established on better promises', 'a new covenant'. Christ, in bringing in the new covenant, has abrogated the old. Why have a new covenant, if the old covenant, the obsolete covenant, is still up and running? What place is there for a covenant that has vanished away? In particular, how can there be three *new*-covenant uses (*à la* Calvin) for something which is obsolete, grown old, and has vanished?

Take Hebrews 9. The same contrast between the covenants is drawn yet again. The old covenant, the law, was done away with at 'the time of reformation' (Heb. 9:10), 'the time of the new order' (NIV); that is, by the work of Christ. And, as far as benefits go, the new covenant is on a totally different plane to the old. The first covenant was all outward, it accomplished no salvation, and it has been done away with. But when we come to the new, how very different the story. God has always required blood sacrifice since 'without [the] shedding of blood there is no remission' (Heb. 9:22). Consequently, in the old covenant, blood was continually offered 'according to the law' (Heb. 9:22); namely, 'the blood of goats and calves... the blood of bulls and goats and the ashes of a heifer' (Heb. 9:12-13). How pointedly this is contrasted with the blood sacrifice of the new covenant, 'the blood of Christ', 'his own blood' (Heb. 9:12-14). Note the double contrast. *First*, the many sacrifices under the law are contrasted with the one sacrifice of Christ (see also Heb. 10:1-4,10-14). *Secondly*, the blood of animals is contrasted with the precious blood of Christ (see also 1 Pet. 1:18-19). What conclusion ought to be drawn from such contrasts? 'How much more shall the blood of Christ... cleanse your conscience from dead works to serve the living God? And for this reason he is the mediator of the new covenant'. It was necessary that Christ should redeem from 'the transgressions under the first covenant' because the first covenant was useless to save. It was more than 'necessary', however; it is the very thing which Christ *did* in bringing in the new (Heb. 9:11-15). How is it possible for covenant theologians to say these covenants are one and the same?

Take Hebrews 10:1-20,28-29.

> For the law, having a shadow of the good things to come, and not the very image of the things... He takes away the first that he may establish the second... The Holy Spirit also witnesses to us; for after he had said before: 'This is the covenant that I will make with them after those days', says the LORD... then he adds: 'Their sins and their lawless deeds I will remember no more'... Anyone who has rejected Moses' law dies without mercy... Of how much worse punishment, do you suppose, will he be thought worthy who has trampled the Son of God underfoot, counted the blood of the covenant by which he was sanctified a common thing, and insulted the Spirit of grace?

Omitting the 'and' in Hebrews 10:1, which is not in the original, the verse reads: 'For the law, having a shadow of the good things to come, not the very image of the things, can never...'. Once again, we have a contrast, and more than a contrast. They – the shadow and the image – were *opposed* to each other. See Colossians 2:17. And the contrast, the opposition, is between the law and the gospel. There is a large, basic, fundamental difference between the two covenants, between the law and the gospel, which difference governs many issues – in particular, the believer and the law. It is the continuity/discontinuity issue once again.

The rest of Hebrews 10 goes on to draw the same contrast between the two covenants, and comes to the same conclusion as earlier passages, but from the opposite point of view; namely, punishment, not mercy. The two covenants both carried punishments, but since the new covenant is superior to the old, it is only to be expected that the punishments under the

new covenant are far more serious than those under the old.[4]
And they certainly are: 'Anyone who has rejected Moses' law
dies without mercy... Of how much worse punishment, do you
suppose, will he be thought worthy who has trampled the Son
of God underfoot, counted the blood of the covenant by which
he was sanctified a common thing, and insulted the Spirit of
grace?' (Heb. 10:28-29). Yes, 'of how much worse
punishment'? How can the covenants be the same? Their
punishments are as different as their benefits.

Hebrews 12:18-29 stresses exactly the same distinction
between the two covenants. The old covenant was physical; the
new is spiritual. Mount Sinai is sharply contrasted with Mount
Zion (Heb. 12:18,22). The old covenant was issued with
burning and blackness, darkness and tempest (Heb. 12:18); the
new is full of joy and happiness. The old brought terror, fear
and trembling – even for Moses (Heb. 12:19-21); the new
brought peace and salvation. The old said: 'Stay away, keep
off' (Heb. 12:20); the new cries: 'Come and welcome'. It is
utterly impossible for these two covenants to be the same.

Isaac Watts:

> *Curs'd be the man, for ever curs'd,*
> *That does one wilful sin commit;*
> *Death and damnation for the first,*
> *Without relief, and infinite.*

> *Thus Sinai roars, and round the earth*
> *Thunder, and fire, and vengeance flings;*
> *But Jesus, thy dear gasping breath*
> *And Calvary, say gentler things:*

> *'Pardon and grace, and boundless love,*
> *Streaming along a Saviour's blood;*
> *And life, and joy, and crowns above,*
> *Obtained by a dear bleeding God'.*

---

[4] As before, the warning passages are real.

Hark! How he prays (the charming sound
Dwells on his dying lips): 'Forgive!'
And every groan and gaping wound
Cries: 'Father, let the rebels live!'

Go, ye that rest upon the law,
And toil and seek salvation there,
Look to the flame that Moses saw,
And shrink, and tremble, and despair.

But I'll retire beneath the cross;
Saviour, at thy dear feet I'll lie!
And the keen sword that justice draws,
Flaming and red, shall pass me by.

The Mosaic covenant was abolished in Christ. And since the Mosaic covenant, the law, has been abolished in Christ, how can it be the perfect rule for the believer? Does the believer live on Mount Zion for justification, and, at the same time, live on Mount Sinai for sanctification? We are expressly told that as believers we have not come to Sinai (Heb. 12:18)![5]

If I may interject a personal note, when I preach the passage, I start by asking the congregation what mountain they are living on. In the discourse, I set out the two mountains in question, and ask them which of the two they are living on. Their answer makes all the difference in the world – and in eternity! Make no mistake! They are living on one of the two – not both! As we all are!

How anybody can read Hebrews and come away with the impression that the law and the gospel are the same covenant, or that believers are under the law as a perfect rule, utterly baffles me.

---

[5] I would not press it, but Heb. 12:18 has all the appearance of destroying preparationism by the law, too.